LAUGHTER AND BLOOD

Manjula Padmanabhan is a writer, artist and playwright. She grew up in Europe and Southeast Asia, and returned to India as a teenager in the late 1960s. The popular comic strip character Suki, created by Manjula, first appeared in print during the 1980s and was recently revived in *The Hindu BusinessLine*, the Chennai-based financial newspaper. In 1997, her play *Harvest* won first place in the Onassis Prize for Theatre in Greece. She is the author of several critically acclaimed books, including *Kleptomania, Three Virgins and Other Stories, Escape, The Island of Lost Girls* and *Hot Death, Cold Soup*. She has also written and illustrated a number of books for children, among them *Mouse Attack* and *Mouse Invaders*, and a series of picture puzzle books.

COLLECTED PLAYS
VOLUME TWO

LAUGHTER AND BLOOD

Performance Pieces

Manjula Padmanabhan

hachette INDIA

First published in 2020 by Hachette India
(Registered name: Hachette Book Publishing India Pvt. Ltd)
An Hachette UK company
www.hachetteindia.com

SRD

See p. 205 for the publication history of the plays in this volume.

ISBN 978-93-89253-36-8

Hachette Book Publishing India Pvt. Ltd
4th & 5th Floors, Corporate Centre,
Plot No. 94, Sector 44, Gurugram 122003, India

Typeset in ITC Legacy Serif Std 10.5/14
by InoSoft Systems, Noida

Printed and bound in India
by Manipal Technologies Limited, Manipal

MIX
Paper from responsible sources
FSC™ C043100

CONTENTS

AUTHOR'S NOTE

In 1984, I had no expectation of being a playwright. That was the year in which I wrote *Lights Out*. A friend had described a shocking incident to me in a way that left an indelible impression. I wanted to write about it, but needed a medium other than fiction or journalism. When a friend suggested writing a play about it, I thought, "Yes. Why not?"

I was 31. I had been supporting myself as a freelance journalist, cartoonist and illustrator for 10 years. I lived as a paying guest, sitting alone at my desk, producing work that would eventually appear in mass-circulation newspapers or magazines. I sometimes heard from the strangers who saw or read my work but I almost never met them.

It was only at the first public reading of *Lights Out* one year later, that I understood how very different it was to be a playwright. The cosy security afforded by an editorial team and publishing establishment was stripped away. I alone was responsible for the words I had written. No one else stood between me and the anger, fear or discomfort I had stirred in the small audience that had gathered for the reading. It was an unfamiliar and vulnerable position to be in. Someone who was there told me later that I looked like an owl blinking in the spotlight, as if I couldn't understand why everyone was looking at me!

Lights Out was unusual in two ways. The first was that it was based directly on a real-life incident. The second was that it got performed relatively quickly after I wrote it. This second fact permitted me to imagine that all plays could, once written, easily find a stage and an audience. Not true! It would be at least 14 years before something new of mine was performed onstage again.

During that time, I wrote three more pieces: *The Mating Game Show*, *The Sextet* and *The Artist's Model*. Of these, *The Mating Game Show* came the closest to being performed. It was the foundation for a TV serial, filmed by Govind Nihalani, during the brief heady period in which BiTV allowed Indian film-makers to dream of a censorship-free TV channel. Alas, when that initiative collapsed, so did the production of *The Mating Game Show*. Though filming was complete and most of the show was edited, it was never broadcast.

In 1996 I wrote my fifth play, *Harvest*. One year later, it won the Onassis Prize for Theatre in Greece. No one had heard of the award because it was the inaugural year of the prize. In 1998, *Harvest* was performed in New Delhi and in early 2000 in Greece. In 2001, Govind Nihalani made *Deham*, a film based on the play. Since then it's been performed, sometimes twice in one year, in different locations around the globe but most often by college theatre groups, most often in the US.

In 2002, I wrote *Hidden Fires*, a set of five monologues loosely inspired by the Gujarat riots. These were published by Seagull, the excellent Kolkata-based publisher that has supported the arts, theatre in particular, for many years. The short performance pieces have since been performed by small theatre groups over the years. Most often, only the first, fourth and fifth. I'm not always informed about performance schedules, so I don't really know.

This brings me to two idiosyncrasies of mine as a playwright. One is that I work alone. While most working playwrights have access to a theatre group with whom they can workshop ideas, for me that has almost never been the case. In part, that's been because without funding or a grant or an establishment (such as a university) with the resources to hold regular rehearsals or even just readings, it's impossible to bring a group of performers together. It is also because I move around a lot, am semi-reclusive and haven't found like-minded people to work with. The result is that I have written all but one of my plays and performance pieces in complete seclusion.

The second idiosyncrasy is that, unlike most people who want to write plays but are frustrated by the thousand obstacles between their desire and the stage, I have just plodded on. With few performances and very little support, I have nevertheless continued to write scripts. This is not a complaint. Theatre really is, in every sense, a difficult discipline to build a career upon. Many people who have the skill and the ambition to be playwrights eventually turn to writing screenplays for TV and cinema.

One reason, perhaps, that I could write plays was because of my comic strips. Whenever I am asked how I gained experience for writing dialogue, I point to my cartoon character Suki and the strips in which she has appeared: "Double Talk" (*Sunday Observer*, Bombay, 1982–86), "Suki" (*Pioneer*, New Delhi, 1992–97) and SukiYaki (*The Hindu BusinessLine*, Chennai, 2016–present). Writing cartoons may also explain why, despite all that is dark and broody in my plays, there's also an element of humour.

Now and then, I have had opportunities to do a reading of my trial runs. Over the years this has resulted in a number of short pieces. This includes one originally called *General Assembly*, which was renamed *Astro-Nuts*, now published as a stand-alone edition. It's an almost-full-length play intended for a young adult audience. Another play began life as five pages written in 1997. It refused to move beyond those five pages however much I pushed and prodded at it until it suddenly sprang up and became a full-length play called *Consequences* in 2015 during a writing residency in the College of Wooster, Ohio, USA.

I first began to think of putting the unpublished plays together in one volume perhaps eight years ago. By this time, I'd been receiving plaintive requests from Indian theatre students desperate for research material. I understand, of course, that this has less to do with quality than simple supply and demand: there aren't many women playwrights anywhere in the world. Fewer still are those whose work is available in print. These students had done their research online. They had noticed references to readings of scripts by me that, unlike *Harvest*, *Lights Out* and *Hidden Fires*, had not appeared in print. So they wrote to me.

I knew that to share an unpublished script by email would be to risk losing all control over it. I refused access. One of these students had declared her thesis subject before realizing that my unpublished plays would not be available to her. I felt terrible about denying access, but there was nothing to be done. All the pieces needed to be worked on before they were print-ready. None had been performed. To share them would be to do myself and the students a disservice.

I continued to withhold the plays, but said I was working on a compendium. Which is, of course, what this two volume set is. Originally, my publisher, Hachette India, and I had not planned to include the already-published plays. However, in the interim, an unexpected development has taken place: a fresh surge of interest in theatre in India. Keeping that in mind, we decided that it made sense to issue all the plays together.

The full-length plays are in *Blood and Laughter*, the shorts in *Laughter and Blood*. I have provided a rough chronology (below), but "rough" means just that. I have continued to tinker with the scripts right until the page-proof stage. For instance, I wrote the first three-hour-long version of *The Mating Game Show* in 1983–84. Since then, I've rewritten it so often that I stopped counting after Mark XX. And that does not include the typewritten screenplays I wrote for the 24-episode TV serial that was doomed never to be seen!

Every single one of these scripts has a story attached to it. Rather than create a single giant introduction to the volumes, I have taken the path of providing brief notes to preface the pieces. Since some of the shorter pieces are in sets, I've focused on the set, rather than on each piece separately.

None of this would have been possible without the warm support and advice of many wonderful friends and editors. Right here in the introduction, however, I'd like to acknowledge six people: Kavita Arora, whose eye-witness account led to *Lights Out*; Rekha Khanna, who said, "Write a play!"; Ranvir Shah, who made the first reading of *Lights Out* possible, on a terrace in Madras; Gulan and Jayant Kripalani, who brought *Lights Out* alive onstage for the first time; and Govind Nihalani, who has supported so many struggling artistes, including me.

These friends were with me from the start. They are still with me, all these many years later. I thank them with all my heart.

Manjula Padmanabhan

CHRONOLOGY OF THE PLAYS

A rough chronology of when the plays were written:

Lights Out	1984
The Mating Game Show	1985 onwards
The Artist's Model	1995
Harvest	1996
Astro-Nuts	2006
Consequences	2014 (completed)

Chronology of the short performance pieces:

The Sextet (set)	early 1990s
Against Her Will	
The Anarchist	
The Man in Their Lives	
Bed Bugs	
The Human Reproductionary Symptom	
Double Solitaire	
The Senses-Taker	circa 2000
The Wish	2001
The Rehearsal	2008
Hidden Fires (set)	2002
Hidden Fires	
Famous Last Words	
Know the Truth!	
Points	
Invocation	

The Cook's Story	2006–08
The Dhobi's Wife	2008
Ladies' Night	2013
The Rape Artist	2013
Blind Date	2019 (completed)
The Organ Speaker	2013 (completed)

Introduction
The Sextet

I wrote this set of six short performance pieces in the early nineties. They were meant to express the irritation I felt towards the type of plays called "Sex Comedies" that were so popular in Indian cities. I had seen a number of these over the years. I found them very funny – yes, of course I did. They were the stage-tested result of decades of fine-tuning from theatres in the UK and the US. My irritation with them arose from my belief that they were all wholly concerned with infidelity. Not sex.

My idea, therefore, was to write six brief pieces that would each focus on some aspect of sexual behaviour. The set would include infidelity but not be confined to it as a theme. The choice of six was merely because the English word for a set of six things begins with the word "sex". I wanted the pieces to be funny but in a brain-tickling sort of way rather than a belly laugh.

I had a few readings in the early days, but it was clear to me that I needed to work on them a bit before I could release them properly. I have tinkered with them over the years, but the time for publishing them as a stand-alone set or even releasing them for a stage performance never came up. This is the first time they will appear together in print.

AGAINST HER WILL
The set-up involves two young men waiting for a young woman to turn up, in the hope of having sex with her. From their conversation, it becomes clear that one of them has an attitude towards sex that would make him extremely unpopular in today's world. The twist in the tale is that the girl, when she turns up, is clearly well ahead of the game.

THE ANARCHIST
Two lovers are in bed, enjoying the warm afterglow of sex. When, however, the young woman reveals that she was only mildly aroused her partner is outraged. He insists that full satisfaction is surely not a choice but a duty. He sets out to prove that he can and will bring her to orgasm. But she manages to slip away, regardless.

The innovation here is that the two performers are wearing what I have dubbed "nude suits". That is, they are fully clothed in outfits that look like jokey versions of nude bodies.

THE MAN IN THEIR LIVES

Two women – one married and middle-aged, the other young and single – meet in the home of the married one. Accompanying them through the scene is the phantom presence of the married woman's husband. An actor in a grey costume takes the role of the phantom husband. He follows the conversation of the two women closely, as the wife reveals to the younger woman that she knows of her husbands many affairs. The spectral husband mimes his reaction to what's said about him. But as one sordid revelation follows another, he's gradually pushed to the periphery of the situation.

BEDBUGS

A mother, her grown son and his new bride are all together in a single large bed. The bride remains under the covers throughout the scene. The young man begins to have sex with his wife, causing the bed springs to squeak. When the mother objects, he explains that he's searching for bedbugs, as usual. The mother accepts this absurd explanation while lamenting the loss of her son to the unseen daughter-in-law. However much she tries to engage him in conversation, she is, of course, doomed to fail.

THE HUMAN REPRODUCTIONARY SYMPTOM

A teacher attempts to teach her three female students about human reproduction. The problem is that the teacher cannot refer directly to any of the terms related to sex. She resorts instead to mangled approximations, growing increasingly infuriated by the girls' inability to understand her. By the time the bell rings to signal the end of class she is wholly incoherent.

DOUBLE SOLITAIRE

A couple settle down at a card table and begin to play a game of double-handed solitaire. And that's it. That's all they do: they laugh and joke and take tremendous pleasure in the shared delight of a game well played.

THE SEXTET

AGAINST HER WILL

Characters

SUNNY

Late twenties. Wage-earner. Thin. Nervy. Hairy.

ROCKY

Baby-faced, techy-type, happy-go-lucky.

HONEY

Friendly, confident twenty-year-old; secretary/molecular biologist/ whatever. Dressed for a casual night out.

Sitting room with two chairs – an easy chair and a straight-backed dining chair without arms – and a settee. SUNNY is sitting in the easy chair. ROCKY is pacing up and down.

SUNNY: For God's sake! Sit down!

ROCKY: I – I'm too nervous!

SUNNY: There's nothing to be nervous about.

ROCKY: When will she come?

SUNNY: (*darkly*) You can never tell with women. They're really good at pretending.

ROCKY: What? Oh! No ... I meant ... when did she *say* she'd get here?

SUNNY: (*looking at his watch*) Ten minutes ago.

ROCKY: (*sits down*) I ... I ... don't think I can go through with this.

SUNNY: Stop *worrying*!

ROCKY: Have *you* ever done it before?

SUNNY: Huh. Of course.

ROCKY: I mean, like ... *this*?

SUNNY: (*deadpan*) Like what?

ROCKY: (*stands up again*) I ... I mean, you know! (*twitches his hands*) Against her will.

SUNNY: Whose will?

ROCKY: You know! The ... girl! Woman. Whatever! The theoretical woman.

SUNNY: Hah! (*darkly*) Women are never theoretical. They're rhetorical. In the extreme!

ROCKY: No, I meant, have you ever ... you know ... taken a woman *against her will*?

SUNNY: Taken a woman *where* against her will?

ROCKY: Oh, come on! You know what I mean. To bed. Against her will. (*he looks embarrassed*)

SUNNY: (*shrugs*) Well, the fact is a woman never goes to bed willingly. With a man, I mean. To have sex. If she isn't married to him. Believes she'll lose respect. They say that times have changed! Haha. This hasn't. Because women don't want to seem wanton.

ROCKY: (*frowning*) Wanting?

SUNNY: Wan*ton*. You know, like the soup in Chinese restaurants. Even when she *is*.

ROCKY: (*seriously confused*) Like *soup*?

SUNNY: Stop playing dumb! You know what I mean!

ROCKY: Honestly I don't! Where does soup ...

SUNNY: Stop, STOP! I referred to soup so that you'd understand that I was saying, wan*ton* not wan*ting*!

ROCKY: Oh. Okay. But why should we suppose that a woman is wanton even when she ISN'T? And suppose *you* want that non-wanton woman who wants you too in the ordinary wanTING way ... (*pauses for breath while looking expectantly at SUNNY*)

SUNNY: Well?

ROCKY: (*sighs in exasperation*) Well! Have you ever taken such a woman ... *against her will*?

SUNNY: (*pause*) You mean ... against her *won't!*

ROCKY: Well, and assuming that her won't is truly neither wan*ton* nor wan*ting* but rather a direct, sincere non-wan*ting* won't!

SUNNY: Look! Why can't you say exactly what *you* want!

ROCKY: Oh! To know if you've ever R-A-P-E-D (*he spells it out*) a woman, for God's sake!

SUNNY: R-A- ...? Oh! No! No, no, no! *Of course* not. I'm not that kind of man. Wouldn't dream of being.

ROCKY: Okay! So ... this *is* your first attempt, then! Tonight?

SUNNY: (*clutching his head*) Bloody hell! That's the whole reason you are here, right? To help with the ropes? And the tying down?

ROCKY: Right. Okay. So ... here's what I'm wondering: d'you think ... I mean ... is it ... *necessary*? This whole ... forcing angle?

SUNNY: Necessary? Well. Probably not. Not these days. But efficient? Yes. More efficient.

ROCKY: (*starts to pace again*) And this woman ... is she ... tall?

SUNNY: (*frowns*) What are you getting at?

ROCKY: I ... I ... was just thinking it might be difficult to get her down, you know, and ...

SUNNY: (*impatiently*) Look! I've already been over it with you! She'll get here, we'll give her a couple of drinks, then I'll stand behind her and tie her arms to the chair! That's all! The rest is up to us!

ROCKY: (*fretfully*) Yes, yes – but – supposing she resists *too much*?

SUNNY: Ohhh ... Didn't I explain it enough? (*jumps up and talks into ROCKY's face*) That's the *whole point*! We *want* her to resist! We *want* her to struggle!

ROCKY: But WHY? Why should we want to hurt her – I thought you said you'd never even dream of –

SUNNY: Who said anything about hurting? We just want her to *struggle*. Or at least *seem* to struggle. So that then we can ... you know ... Have Our Way With Her. But without the least *question* of hurting her. Or outraging her modesty. Or any of those ghastly things. No, no, not at all. Never. All we want is a little, minor, non-painful, non-aggressive, possibly even enjoyable and wholly consensual ... *forcing*.

ROCKY: Are you saying you want the woman to *agree* to being forced?

SUNNY: Exactly. That is exactly what I'm saying.

ROCKY: And the reason for this...?

SUNNY: (*exasperated*) We've BEEN through all this! I explained it! (*as if to a child*) The reason it has to seem forced and she HAS to resist is that otherwise ... (*throws his arms up theatrically to emphasize his point*) otherwise it becomes Love! Romance! Commitment! Marriage! (*puts his arms down*) And all for the sake of a ... a ... two-second spasm.

ROCKY: (*automatically*) ... three-second.

SUNNY: (*archly*) Oh? *Three* seconds, is it? Well, well! Aren't you the lucky man! And I thought you said you'd never had sex?

ROCKY: (*primly*) Not in ... in ... *company*.

SUNNY: That's a funny name for a girl. Company!

Just then the doorbell rings. Both men jump.

ROCKY: (*whispers*) Oo! Must be her!

SUNNY: (*slicking his hair back, also whispering*) Now, just relax, okay? If we're tense she might become suspicious and refuse to drink!

ROCKY: What'll we do then?

SUNNY: Can't you stop with your worries? Just relax. Everything will be fine. I'm going to open the door, okay?

Goes offstage. Sound of door opening.

HONEY: Sunny – hi! Am I late?

SUNNY: Not at all, not at all! (*admiring tone*) Mmmm! Aren't we looking wonderful!

ROCKY writhes comically, striking a different "relaxed" pose each time.

Enter SUNNY.

SUNNY: (*over his shoulder*) Come in, come in!

Enter HONEY.

HONEY: (*walks straight on to centre stage. Looks around appraisingly*) Not bad. Interesting. Good solid furniture. Could do with some art though. And a dog. D'you have a dog? (*suddenly notices ROCKY, reclining at an unnatural angle across the settee*) Oh! Hello? Who's this?

ROCKY leaps up as if he's been electrocuted, sticking his hand out, as if in greeting.

ROCKY: (*practically shouting*) Hi! I'm Relaxed!

SUNNY, behind HONEY, groans silently and rolls his eyes.

I ... I mean, totally calm ... cool!

SUNNY: (*slipping in between them*) Honey, this is my friend Rocky.

HONEY: (*smiles kindly*) He certainly is!

ROCKY: How about a DRINK? I can make you drink. Drunk. I mean, I can make you something to drunk. I mean ...

HONEY: (*amused surprise*) I'm sure you don't have to *make* me ...

SUNNY: (*cursing silently while the other two talk*) He means he can *offer* you something to *drink*.

HONEY: (*smiles, shrugs*) I know! I got it. Sure. Just give me a moment. Okay?

SUNNY: (*propels HONEY towards the armchair*) Honey, here. Why don't you take a seat?

ROCKY: (*recognizing that the chair will be useless from the perspective of tying up*)

No! There's no point sitting in *that* one – sit here!

See? It has this nice straight back! (*pats the back of the chair*)

HONEY: (*poised between both chairs*) Oh stop. I hate being forced into anything! I prefer the sofa anyway!

She steps towards the sofa and settles herself into it. SUNNY, taking his cue, quickly goes across and sits next to her. She smiles at him. ROCKY looks daggers at SUNNY then sits down on the chair intended for HONEY. Continues trying to look relaxed.

HONEY: (*to SUNNY but including ROCKY*) So ... three's company tonight, huh?

SUNNY: I hope you don't feel crowded?

ROCKY: How about that drink?

HONEY: (*stretching languidly*) Ohhh ... not just yet. I never have a drink ...

The two men exchange panicked glances.

... before sex!

SUNNY and ROCKY: Before *sex*? My goodness ... who said anything about sex?

SUNNY: (*to ROCKY*) Did you mention sex, by any chance?

ROCKY: No, I didn't –

HONEY: (*laughing delightedly*) Oh! How funny you two are! (*she looks at them a moment as if inviting them to be frank with her*)

Come on! Isn't that why I'm here tonight?

Silence.

HONEY: (*starting to take her shoes off*) Don't tell me you didn't discuss it. Because I won't believe you.

The two men look furtively at one another and then quickly away.

HONEY: Hey! Listen, you guys! I want it too, right? (*shrugs good-naturedly*) I mean, I thought it was going to be just Sunny but you're okay too, Rocky! (*she pats the settee*) So, who's first?

SUNNY: Well, uh ... look, no reason to rush, okay?

ROCKY: (*tugging at his collar*) I ... I need a drink!

HONEY: (*earnestly*) You really shouldn't have one, Rocky! Alcohol really ruins a man's ability to perform!

SUNNY: Ah ... look, we've only just met. How about we wait to build up some atmosphere?

HONEY: Oh, come *on*! That's so old-fashioned! Why waste time?

ROCKY: (*looking a whole lot happier*) She's got a point, Sunny! After all, wasn't that what YOU were interested in? Efficiency?

SUNNY: (*sits down abruptly*) Well ... the problem is ... I can't! Don't you see? (*appealing to ROCKY, though he knows it's hopeless*) If she's willing then ... then ... (*shrugs helplessly*) how can we force her?

HONEY: Oh – that's *easy*! I can *pretend* to be unwilling! I'm good at pretending!

ROCKY: Yes! (*to SUNNY*) How about that? Won't that be all right?

SUNNY: (*miserably*) We can give it a try.

ROCKY: (*to HONEY*) Well, look, we were planning to tie you up –

SUNNY wants to prevent ROCKY from revealing everything, but flops back, defeated.

HONEY: *Tie me up?* (*she seems delighted with the prospect*) Ooh! What fun! I've never done that sort of thing before!

SUNNY: (*groaning, to no one in particular*) You see? She's ruining everything!

ROCKY: Yah! And then, while you kick and struggle –

HONEY: – and scream? May I scream as well?

ROCKY: (*looking towards SUNNY*) Sunny? Is it all right? Will the neighbours object?

SUNNY: Oh, what does it matter! Scream away!

ROCKY: (*to HONEY*) Right! So let's get started! Honey?

She leaps up and settles down in the designated chair, wriggling in anticipation.

HONEY: Oooh! This is such fun! (*leans back so that ROCKY, who has picked up the rope from under the settee, can tie her arms back*) Like this?

ROCKY: (*concentrating on the knots*) Uhh ... one moment, one moment ... hope I'm not hurting you? Okay ... see if you can pull – yes, great. Okay, now ... the other side? Just loop through – see it's already knotted! Great! You're a natural, Honey. Sure you've not done this before? Okay! Ready, Sunny! (*SUNNY is looking away, a pained expression on his face*) Sunny?

HONEY: Rocky, how about threatening me a little? Like in the movies, you know?

ROCKY: Great idea! (*stands, leering lecherously, his hands outstretched to grab her*) Arrhhhhhh! Heh! Heh! Heh! (*wild parody*) Now my juicy little mango! Let's see if you're as ripe as you look!

HONEY: (*recoiling, squealing like a piglet*) Nooooooo! Please! Don't touch me! Don't hurt me! I'll do whatever you say – but *don't hurt me*! (*paddling her legs*) Mummmaaaaaa!

ROCKY: (*snarling*) Quiet, slut! There's only one way to deal with women like you and that's –

SUNNY: (*cutting in*) STOP! Stop it. You're behaving like a pair of schoolchildren!

HONEY: (*grinning*) Wow! You must have been to some very weird school!

SUNNY: (*ignoring HONEY's remark*) Be reasonable! A woman who's willing cannot be raped! It becomes the *other thing*!

ROCKY: But ... so what? (*looking fondly at HONEY*) Honey's not going to fall in love or want to get married or anything – are you, Honey?

HONEY: *Married!* (*scornfully*) To two guys I've just met? Huh! *Of course* not!

SUNNY: Oh, that's what they *always* say! (*leaping to his feet*) So! You get into bed with them, and you thrash about for an hour or so! After which you wash up and maybe even drop them home! And you congratulate yourself for having found, for once, a woman who doesn't fondle your credit cards before she drops her panties! And then a couple of weeks later your secretary tells you, with a smirk all over her face, that someone called to say that she was pregnant and ... (*falsetto voice*) "What should I do now?" (*swats at the air violently*) Ahh! They're all the same! Scheming, cunning, cold-hearted ...

HONEY: You don't use contraceptives?

ROCKY: Supposing we all sign contracts?

SUNNY: What? And provide the lady with legal proof? Forget it! She might already be pregnant with someone else's bastard!

HONEY: (*mildly petulant*) Guys, guys, if you want to spend the whole night arguing, that's fine – but I'd like to go find someone else to have fun with!

ROCKY: (*greatly saddened at this thought*) Sunny, Sunny, she's all tied up and everything! Why don't we all just have our two or three seconds of bliss and at least get *that* done?

SUNNY: And that's another thing! If it's all consensual and happy-boppy then your two seconds is more likely to be two *hours*! And panting! And wailing! And (*falsetto*) ... "Not yet, Sunny, not yet!" And stopping to drink cold milk! And hammering on with your teeth clenched! And doing quadratic equations in your head! And losing your ... your ... concentration! And reviving yourself again with thoughts of Sunny Leone! And on and on and on until you're numb from the waist down and your shoulder muscles are on fire ... so much so that, by the time Her Ladyship finally detonates, your precious two seconds feel like a single shot from a cap pistol beside a neutron bomb! (*to the world at large*) It's not worth it, I tell you, it's not worth it!

During this speech, HONEY frees herself from her bonds. She straightens up.

HONEY: (*goes to SUNNY, puts out her arm as if to place it around his shoulders*) You know, Sunny –

SUNNY: (*reacting violently*) Aaahhh! Stay away from me! Get away, get away!

HONEY: (*shrugging extravagantly*) Well ... I *tried*.

Gives ROCKY a quick peck on the cheek and exits.

ROCKY: (*waves to HONEY's back then turns on SUNNY*) See what you've done! An excellent lady – *gone*! All because of you!

SUNNY: (*pensively*) You know ... there was a time when all you had to do was glance in a girl's direction and she would wilt before your eyes! Covered in sweet confusion. Ahh, *those* were the days. The *good* days. A man strolled the streets like a musician and every girl, a string for him to pluck. Just a glance ... a wink ... a chirp from his lips ... was enough. The girls would duck their dear little heads, cover their faces, cry out in bright fluting voices. Like pretty, delicate birds! Fluttering like butterflies. (*shakes his head sadly*) But no more. They're free now. They're loose in the world. They've thrown their strings away.

ROCKY: (*sits down, dejected*) I don't know about all that. But you're wrong about Honey. *I* think she was really *nice*. Decent. She just wanted to have a good time. For one night.

Spotlight over SUNNY as the rest of the stage darkens.

SUNNY: Don't be taken in, Rocky. These modern hussies! These jiggle-breasted Amazons with their ... their ... steaming underarms, pierced navels and unshaven legs! Their lusts and insatiable needs!

They've killed romance, I tell you! They've cut its throbbing heart out, stabbed it with their sex manuals and smothered it with contraceptive gels.

They've reduced us men from the thunder-throated gods we used to be, to nothing more than the sum of our inches. A frail, uncertain rod of rigid tissue, astride of which they bay and howl like things possessed! They've lost their ancient fear of us!

And we ... our simple joy of them.

Lights fade and curtain.

THE ANARCHIST

Bedroom. In semi-darkness, two people, JOYA and RAKESH, covered by their bed sheets are lying entangled in bed. They are meant to be naked, but what we actually see is that both actors are wearing full-length, loose-fitting bodysuits, buttoned at the shoulders. Preferably, they are in bright contrasting colours – one red, one green, for example – with the major sexual organs either painted on or sewn on as pouches in such a manner as to look comical, and embellished with copious fake pubic hair. They should look like cartoon figures of a nude woman and man.

RAKESH: (*stirring and stretching deliciously*) Mmmmmmm! (*reaches up to look at the alarm clock. Flops back. Turns towards JOYA and puts his arm around her*)

That was good!

JOYA: (*not turning around, inarticulate grunt*) Nnnngg.

RAKESH: Wasn't it?

JOYA: Ng.

RAKESH: (*nonplussed. He settles back briefly to confer with himself. Something is wrong. Turns back to her, shaking her a little*) Well? Didn't you like it? Didn't you have a good time?

JOYA: Ng!

RAKESH: (*now thoroughly disturbed. Leans back on his elbows a moment, frowning, before turning back to her and shaking her again*) Speak to me!

JOYA: (*turning around in a sudden explosive movement, with a great hissing of sheets, so that she is now fully awake, facing RAKESH, supported on one elbow, her chest covered for modesty's sake, by the sheet*) Listen, do you mind? I'm trying to get some sleep!

She settles down, burrowing into the sheets and under a pillow, but facing him now.

RAKESH: (*looks at her a moment. Then sits all the way up. He looks like a bear with a toothache. Turns around so that his body faces the audience, his sheet wound loosely about his lower trunk, his head turned back towards JOYA. Prods her belligerently on the shoulder*) You can't do this to me!

JOYA: (*from under the pillow, muffled*) Do what to you?

RAKESH: Insult me like this!

JOYA: (*still muffled*) What?

RAKESH: (*with a martyred expression on his face*) I have my pride, you know!

JOYA: (*finally brings her head up, wincing against the light*) What are you talking about?

RAKESH: (*belligerently*) If you didn't have an orgasm it wasn't my fault!

JOYA: (*tiredly*) Who said it was?

RAKESH: (*exploding*) There! You see? You admitted it! You didn't have one!

JOYA: (*looking heavenward and sighing*) Oh ... so what!

She lies back, with pillows to support her head and shoulders.

RAKESH: (*leaping up so that he is crouching on all fours*) So, everything! Listen! I work hard to be a good lover, okay? So I don't want to hear any limp-wristed excuses! The problem with you is you don't make an effort! You don't try hard enough!

JOYA: (*making an irritated face*) Supposing I don't want to?

RAKESH: Hah! (*punches the air*) Hah! That's a good one! That's a great one! That's the best one I've heard in a long time! (*to the world at large, mimicking her*) Supposing I don't want to? Don't be ridiculous! Everyone wants to!

JOYA: (*bored*) Well, I don't. I think it's highly overrated.

RAKESH: (*to the audience*) Will you listen to that? She says the greatest pleasure known to humans is OVERRATED! (*to her*) Say, what are you, anyway? A freak? A moron?

JOYA: (*looks at him for a fraction of a second, before starting to get up and out of bed*) No. Just bored.

RAKESH: (*his reactions get ever more extreme*) Bored? We've just made love and you can tell me that it leaves you bored! You know what that does to me? What it does to my ego? I mean, there's a mean world out there, and I need all the self-esteem I can get, just to put my tie on and face the jungle!

During this speech, JOYA has wandered around looking for something which she finally finds on top of the television – a packet of cigarettes.

JOYA: (*coolly*) So what d'you want to do about it?

Takes out a cigarette and starts to light it.

RAKESH: Well, I'd say you owe it to me to get right back into bed and let me show you what you've been missing!

JOYA: (*comes back to the side of the bed and looks at him, hands on her hips*) Missing? (*turns and sits down, demurely, despite her state of undress*) Don't be silly, Rax! You can't force me to enjoy myself!

RAKESH: (*leering erotically*) You bet I can, baby! I spent two years in the US of A, remember? I know every trick under the blanket!

In a quick move, he grabs her and starts to stroke her "breasts" violently.

Be a good girl now, lie back and we'll have you moaning in no time –

JOYA: (*struggling in his grasp*) Let – me – GO! (*pulls free. Adjusts her nude-suit. Puffs angrily on her cigarette before speaking*) If there's anything I hate, it's this – this – (*she breaks off, unable to find words to express herself*) *compulsory* pleasure! Why can't

I choose when and how I want my pleasure? Including *if* I want my pleasure?

RAKESH: (*watching her like a snake*) You're frigid. Aren't you?

JOYA: (*without much heat*) No. I'm not.

RAKESH: So what's the story, huh? Raped in childhood by your maternal uncle? You went to a convent where they told you that Girls Who Enjoy It Don't Go To Heaven? What is it? What went wrong?

JOYA: (*sighing*) Nothing! There's nothing wrong! (*she settles down*) Why don't you believe me?

RAKESH: (*with deep conviction*) Because it's not normal not to want orgasms! It's like not wanting cars ... or colour televisions. Not natural! Not patriotic! Why, if people went around not wanting orgasms, pretty soon they wouldn't want anything – and then what would happen? World trade would grind to a halt! Governments would collapse! Populations would dwindle! And chaos would rule the earth!

JOYA: (*makes a face*) Don't you think you're getting a little carried away?

RAKESH: (*excitedly*) You're an anarchist, that's what you are! You want to destroy civilization with your monumental indifference!

JOYA: (*indignantly*) No, I'm not! I'm not thinking about civilization or anything else. I'm just ...

RAKESH: (*cutting in*) But there you have it! You're an anarchist without even knowing it!

A silence falls between them.

RAKESH: I'm sorry, Joya, but –

He suddenly lunges for her.

JOYA: (*leaping up just in time*) NO! Rax! Behave yourself!

RAKESH launches himself off the bed, intending to land on JOYA but she eludes him.

RAKESH: Not when all humanity is at stake! Forgive me, Joya! I'm not doing this for myself. I'm doing it for everybody else, for everything we care about – for freedom – for peace – for –

During this speech, he chases her up and down and all around the room. Ultimately, while attempting to cross the bed, she sprawls full length whereupon he leaps on her back, triumphantly.

RAKESH: (*getting into position, with JOYA underneath but still struggling forward. They are both panting hard*) culture – for religion – for god – for democracy – for love, dammit – LOVE – (*in a breathy aside*) Would you mind keeping still just a minute?

JOYA unbuttons her nude-suit and even as RAKESH begins to mount her, has wriggled out from the top of the suit and down the front of the bed, on to the floor and completely out of his grasp. She is fully clothed under the nude-suit. She goes and sits to one side in an armchair, facing the bed. She is more exasperated than ever.

RAKESH: (*apparently unaware that he has only an empty nude-suit under him*) Ahh! That's it! How's that feel, darling? Good, huh? Yeah! Good! Now let's hear a little accompaniment from you, shall we?

JOYA: (*from where she sits, she clears her throat and then with an utterly bored expression on her face, begins to gasp and wheeze*) Uhh! Uhh! Uhh!

RAKESH: (*pumping away like a dog*) Oh, that's it, baby! That's how it should be! That's how it was meant to be! Oo! Yeah! Yeah! Yeah!

For the next couple of minutes, RAKESH ravishes the empty nude-suit, throwing it up in the air, twirling it about himself, passing it under his legs, leaping all over the room with it ... grunting ecstatically, while JOYA, sitting on the armchair and utterly composed, yodels away. Soon enough, with loud screams they both achieve a climax.

RAKESH: (*collapsing face forward on to the bed*) Mmmmmhhh! Ohhhhh! My God! That was really something, huh? Mmmmmmhhhh! Whoo! Hmmmm!

His breathing gradually approaches normal. He sleeps briefly. JOYA watches him, then gets up, gently extracts her suit from under him, folds it up and packs it away into an overnight bag. Then she picks up her packet of cigarettes, finds her shoes and tiptoes out of the room. A few moments later, RAKESH starts to wake up.

RAKESH: (*sleepily reaching out to where he expects to find JOYA*) Mmmmm! Mmmmmmm! That was good! (*pause*) Wasn't it? (*his arm, has begun to register that she is nowhere to be felt. It gropes in an ever wider circle, becoming increasingly frantic*) Wasn't it? Hey! (*with a bounding start he wakes all the way up*) Joya? Joya! Where are you! Come back, goddammit, come back, come back ...

The lights dim and fade out. Curtain.

THE MAN IN THEIR LIVES

Mid-morning, interior. Expensively appointed drawing room in a high-rise building. SWARA is sitting on a settee, looking impatiently at her watch. A low table is set with a tea tray. On the settee, next to SWARA is a loose-leaf binder. SWARA is well dressed, wearing discreet jewellery and is pleasant to look at, in her mid-forties. The lady of the house and used to wealth.

The doorbell rings. She hesitates a moment. Then she goes to the door, at stage right. In walks CECILIA, young, bouncy and obviously dressed to meet a man. She's carrying a bunch of flowers.

Along with CECILIA a man wearing a grey tracksuit enters the room, right behind her. Neither SWARA nor CECILIA acknowledges his presence by looking at him or speaking to him. He can touch CECILIA, and she responds to the touch, but doesn't look directly at him.

He is Swara's HUSBAND. In his fifties, well built, good-looking. He dominates the scene with his silent presence and his mimed antics, as he responds to what the women say. The directions in the script are intended as suggestions, not directives. The actor must find his way into the role, without altering the intention of the script.

CECILIA: (*the door opens in such a way that she cannot immediately see who has opened it*) Helloooo! It's meee – (*gasps*) OH!

HUSBAND enters directly behind CECILIA. He grimaces when he sees SWARA.

SWARA: (*shutting the door*) Hi. I'm Swara.

Makes a rude face at SWARA.

CECILIA: (*unsure whether to brazen it out or not*) Oh ... God.

Puts his arms protectively around CECILIA.

SWARA: (*smiling slightly*) You're ... Cecilia, right?

Mimes an elaborate welcome.

CECILIA: (*deciding to wriggle out*) Listen, I – I – think I've come to the wrong house –

Swatting at SWARA.

SWARA: (*calmly*) No, you haven't –

Looks extravagantly bored.

CECILIA: No, I have an appointment to meet someone and he's –

Mimes pulling her to the door.

SWARA: (*tranquilly*) Yes. I know. I read his note to you.

Pulls a shamefaced grimace.

CECILIA: (*taken off her guard, confirms that she's guilty*) Oh – ! Then you know that I – that we –

Covers his eyes with his hands.

SWARA: (*starts to lead CECILIA inside, towards the seating area to the right*) I've known for a long time. Ever since it started. Won't you come this way?

Mimes to CECILIA not to follow SWARA.

CECILIA: (*starts to go in the indicated direction, then pulls back*) No! I mean, I – I – shouldn't be here!

Pulls her away.

SWARA: (*tilts her head*) Look, I already know. I'm not angry. I won't be nasty to you.

Pretends to wipe her off, as if from a blackboard.

CECILIA: (*suspicious*) But ... what d'you want from me?

Pulls an exaggeratedly suspicious face.

SWARA: (*sits down. Straightens a cushion*) I just ... want to talk to you.

Mimes his disbelief.

CECILIA: (*takes a step forward, which brings her to just behind the armchair*) What ... about?

Tries to pull her away, pleading comically, on bended knee, hand over his heart.

SWARA: (*looks up sharply as if it's obvious*) About him, of course!

Reels as if he's been shot.

CECILIA: (*undecided*) About *him*? What about him?

Looks questioningly.

SWARA: (*looks up at CECILIA, appraising her*) What you see in him. What he is to you ...

Pretends to examine himself.

CECILIA: (*looking down, embarrassed*) I can't do that. I can't do that! You mustn't ask me to! (*she glances at the older woman*) That would be ...

Grins widely, sticks his tongue out at SWARA, thumbs his nose at her.

SWARA: (*quietly*) Disloyal? Yes ... I suppose it would.

Appears to be listening, but in a sneering way.

CECILIA: (*in a rush of feeling*) I – I – can guess what you feel but ... but it all happened so suddenly! I couldn't help myself – we couldn't help ourselves! You must believe me –

As if surrendering to passion, sweeps CECILIA backwards in a deep embrace.

SWARA: (*earnestly*) I do. It's quite easy to believe you. After all ... (*stops*)

Scowls deeply. He guesses what's about to come.

CECILIA: (*there's a hint of glass in her voice*) What –

Shuts her ears for her.

SWARA: (*smiles a little awkwardly and tucks a stray hair back into place*)

Well, I ... (*decides to try a new tack*) Look. Why don't you sit down? I think we may have a lot to say to one another. If you'll just give me a chance –

Tries to stand between CECILIA and SWARA, but doesn't succeed.

CECILIA: (*reluctantly*) Okay, but I won't stay for long!

Holds CECILIA back.

SWARA: (*relaxing*) Thank you. Good. I'm glad. (*an appraising glance*) You know, I've often wanted to do this.

Grimaces. Holds his head in despair.

CECILIA: (*ill at ease*) Do what?

Mimes "DON'T ASK!"

SWARA: (*reaching for the tea cosy, taking it off, not looking at CECILIA as she speaks*) Meet one of his lady friends.

Swats in SWARA's direction.

CECILIA stiffens.

Tries to tell her not to listen.

SWARA: You're the first one. That I've met, I mean. (*she has finished pouring the tea. Reaches for the milk*) Milk?

Looks utterly innocent.

CECILIA: (*very tense*) Uhh ... yes. Thanks. Wh-what do you mean?

Covers his eyes, as if unable to bear what is coming.

SWARA: (*unperturbed*) Sugar? I've never met any of the others.

Mimes shutting SWARA up.

CECILIA: (*she is clutching her flowers defensively. She answers mechanically*) Thanks, yes. Two spoons. Thanks.

Clutching his head in despair.

Crockery clinks as SWARA puts in the sugar, stirs slowly and hands the cup to CECILIA, then pours tea into her own cup.

Mimes frustration.

CECILIA: (*stiffly*) What d'you mean, "others"?

Begs her not to ask.

SWARA: (*shrugs, estimating*) Other women. Maybe ten or twelve. Not counting you.

Mimes "Who me?"

CECILIA: (*she's starting to crack*) T-Twelve?

Mimes vomiting.

SWARA: (*stirs her cup*) Before you, that is ...

Shakes his fist at SWARA.

CECILIA: (*her hand flies up to her mouth, the flowers still cradled in the crook of her arm. The tea is in the other hand, and she puts the cup down now, abruptly*) Ohh!

Flinches.

She reaches for a handkerchief, but SWARA hands her a box of tissues from the table.

CECILIA: The bastard! (*she sobs*)

As if he's been shot.

SWARA: (*settling back with her cup*) Yes. He is, actually. That's why I wanted to meet one of you. I wanted to understand what he has that's so attractive –

As if he's sick to the stomach.

CECILIA: (*still weeping, but the anger is gaining ground*) The BASTARD!

Reeling, as if shot again.

SWARA: My theory is that it's his boyishness. He's always so enthusiastic! So ready to jump up and drive off to the beach or get tickets to the theatre or ...

Tries to claw at SWARA's face.

CECILIA: (*blowing her nose*) I HATE him!

Reels in shock.

SWARA: (*calmly*) Well, he can be very charming. When he wants to be! He knows so much!

CECILIA: (*viciously*) He's a lousy lover!

Looks deeply hurt.

SWARA: (*tiny pause*) Oh ... really? I always just assumed that he must be better when he's with other women.

Slashes in her direction.

CECILIA: (*vehemently*) He's awful! He can't perform unless he's sloshed – and once he is, he just wants to ram it in and whoosh! Over before it's even begun!

Looks down towards his crotch.

SWARA: (*almost laughs*) Why do you like him then?

Looks proud of himself.

CECILIA: (*overcome with a fresh gust of sobs*) Because ... because ... he's so sweet otherwise! He sends me chocolates and he remembers my birthday and he's always so comfortable to be with, really like a – a –

Suggests that it's because of love.

SWARA: (*innocently*) – father?

Snarls in her direction.

CECILIA: Yes! Like a father! A big ... cuddly ... safe ... (*she succumbs to her tears for a couple of moments. Finally raises her head, wiping her nose*) I guess that's why it feels so terrible to hear that there is someone else ... it's like being betrayed by your own father! By a man you've trusted all your life ... (*in a small subdued voice*) I feel I've known him all my life ... (*hiccups a couple of times*) ... but I – I'd started to suspect something. I guess, subconsciously, I knew something had changed. That there was someone else ... (*looks at SWARA with big trusting eyes*) You know who she is?

Feigns disinterest.

SWARA: (*carefully*) I've seen pictures. She lives somewhere off Nepean Sea Road –

Mimes boredom.

CECILIA: (*hearing this covers her face with her hands*) God! GOD! That's where he's been coming from these last few weeks! Fresh from seeing her! And I even smelt her perfume on him the other day and – and – I teased him about it and – and – he said it was this new aftershave he'd got ... Ohhh! He's lied to me! He's lied ... so much! (*another bout of sobbing*) I don't know how you can bear to live with him, knowing all of this!

Goes to her and stands protectively behind her.

SWARA: (*looking down into her teacup*) Well. It's been difficult, at times. Most of the time, actually. I used to be wild with jealousy. I used to watch him, humming to himself as he shaved in the morning, and I used to burn. Thinking about the other women who shared these same intimacies with him. (*drains the cup*)

Looks holy.

CECILIA: (*subdued, clutching her flowers*) You must hate me, too.

Whispers in her ear.

SWARA: (*starts to say something, changes her mind, says another thing instead*) No. No, I don't. Something happened. One day, I suddenly understood it. (*looks intently at CECILIA*) I suddenly understood that I wasn't seeing you as a person. I was seeing you as a thing. His thing. And that if I could only manage to see you as a person, someone who was as easy to hurt and as in need of love as me – then maybe I could reach out to you and we could ... we could ... I don't know! Be friends, maybe.

He weeps, he screams, he cries.

CECILIA: (*frowning, uncertain*) Friends?

He pats her on the head, as if cuddling a baby.

SWARA: (*shrugs*) I could send you chocolates too, you know! After all, it's only his secretary who does it for him! You realize that, don't you?

Laughs at SWARA's suggestion.

CECILIA: (*tries to smile*) Yeah ... I guess ... (*her face crumples up again*) But it's not – it wouldn't be the same! Would it?

Whispers to CECILIA.

(*sobs. Suddenly, she questions SWARA's motives*)

Now he is able to touch her.

No! It wouldn't! Nothing will be the same! Why did you tell me? You shouldn't have! Oh – I don't want to know! I don't! I don't! (*sobs*) If you hadn't told me, at least I'd have my illusions! – at least I could have gone on seeing him – better than not seeing him at all! (*sobs*) I'm not you! I'm not surrounded by him, like you are – by his wealth, his influence. (*pause*) He's ... he's like a warm cloak! When I'm with him – and I'm so cold without him! I need him so much and now you've – you've – TORN him away!

Holds her tight in his embrace, his expressions and gestures closely following the spirit and intention of her speech.

(*sobs*)

He kisses her, caresses her.

And you're just sitting there! So damn smug! On his sofa! In his house! Tearing my life to shreds! (*sobs*)

Holds her tight, seeming in the throes of passion.

I'm not going to leave him! Not! Not! (*sobs*)

Cradles her, rocks her.

You don't know what it's like – to be young – to share rooms with two other girls – to be just a secretary in some big company – and then to have someone like ... like ... HIM to pick you up in his car! And to take you out dancing! And – and – and – to be KIND to you.

CECILIA allows herself to be entirely engulfed by him as he makes faces at SWARA over CECILIA's heaving shoulder.

(*choking with tears*)

His head is buried comfortably in CECILIA's neck.

You don't know any of that – DO YOU!

Pats her as if comforting a child.

She puts her head in her hands, her shoulders shaking with the force of her unhappiness. She reaches for the tissues, three at once, to blow her nose. She composes herself. Only now does she put down the flowers. Then she sits with her arms wrapped about herself as if feeling cold.

Caresses her, warms her up.

SWARA: (*waiting till she's sure that the storm has subsided*) More tea?

Swats in SWARA's direction.

CECILIA: (*her voice is husky*) How did you know about me?

Makes shushing gestures, as if preventing a child from speaking.

SWARA: (*tiny pause*) A detective told me –

He looks up, aghast.

CECILIA: (*looks up, startled*) What?

He holds his hands tight against her ears. But CECILIA pushes his hands away.

SWARA: (*shrugs, smiles slightly*) I was desperate. It had become a sort of obsession with me. My life was filled with phantoms who left lipstick marks on cigarette butts, faded roses squashed in his suit pocket, tiny lace hankies in his briefcase. So, one day I hired a detective. Just like that. And in a couple of weeks, he came back. With names. Dates. Places. Photographs. It was so simple. (*looks thoughtful*)

It changed my life. I felt like a blind person whose eyes had been healed by surgery ... Suddenly, I could see everything. I realized how silly it was to feel jealous of his girls, because I could see how little he gave and how much he got.

As SWARA talks, gradually, once more, CECILIA's body repels his attempts to hold her.

CECILIA: (*cutting in*) But you didn't do anything about it?

He finally has to get up and stand away from CECILIA.

SWARA: (*shrugs*) No. Why should I? All I really wanted was to know the truth – and now I know it! Every two weeks the detectives bring me fresh information and I go through it like reading a magazine, a continuously unfolding serial.

CECILIA: (*her eyes goggling*) You mean – he doesn't know at all? And you're still doing this? With his own money?

For the first time, he looks serious.

SWARA: (*nods, smiles*) Yes.

CECILIA: (*looks at her a moment and then suddenly giggles*) For how long?!

He goes to a corner and sulks.

SWARA: (*considers*) Ohh ... maybe three years, four years –

CECILIA: (*sucks in her breath*) Four years! Don't they mind? The detectives?

He withdraws to himself.

SWARA: (*shrugs*) What do they care? It's just a job, I pay them well and it's not difficult or dangerous.

CECILIA: But then what about me? Why did you decide to tell me?

He looks very melancholy.

SWARA: (*looks carefully at Cecilia*) I thought you seemed like a person I could like. I liked the things you said. I liked the way you looked. I thought for once he had chosen someone I could approve of. Then he began to go out with this new girl. Suddenly, I was angry. I knew what was going to happen. I've seen it happen four, five times already. The tears, the anger, the pleading, the humiliation ... (*pause*) I didn't want to see you broken and helpless. I just suddenly thought, what the hell! He doesn't really hold all the cards! There's at least one card in my hand that I can play. So I've played it! (*she sits forward*) Do you understand? I knew that nothing I said would shake his hold on you as much as just ... *knowing.*

CECILIA: (*she thinks a moment, before saying impulsively*) Can I see the report?

For the rest of the scene HUSBAND wanders about the room, looking at things, pretending not to pay any attention to what the women are saying, but every so often looking over at them with a kind of sadness. He is totally cut out of their circle.

SWARA: (*handing her the file which has been on the sofa beside her*) Of course.

CECILIA opens the file and starts to leaf through the pages. She hasn't been reading long before she smiles a little. Then she laughs softly. SWARA, watching her, smiles as well.

CECILIA: (*a sudden snort of real laughter*) Did you see this? They're talking in the lift? And he says he's never met anyone so intelligent and perceptive. God! What a phony!

SWARA nods, smiling.

CECILIA: And here, look! They're even sitting in the same place at the Rendezvous where he used to take me! He's giving her something – I bet it's the same perfume he gave me – he must have bought it by the gallon! Oh God! I hate him!

Despite her words, there is no pain in her voice any longer. The husband, who has been skulking further and further away from the two women, during these last few lines has finally reached the door. He opens it and exits, taking care to make no noise as he does so.

SWARA: (*as the door closes, starts as if at a sudden sound. Looks around, towards the door, but sees nothing*) That's odd – I thought I heard a door being slammed ... (*turns to CECILIA*) Did you hear it?

Lights fade out.

CECILIA: No. Didn't hear a thing.

Curtain.

BEDBUGS

A bedroom, lit only by the moonlight coming in through the window. The room is dominated by a giant bed. There are three people in the bed, SUKHESH, AYESHA and MA but when the curtain opens none of the occupants are visible except as indistinct lumps under the sheets. AYESHA is never seen.

MA is on the extreme right of the bed. SUKHESH and AYESHA are both huddled to the left. SUKHESH wears a mulmul kurta. MA wears a sari petticoat and blouse with a satin dressing gown over it. Her long white hair is plaited neatly. She sleeps wearing glasses. When she addresses either of the other two, she does not look at them, but straight ahead.

Presently, the sound of rhythmically squeaking bed springs can be heard.

MA: (*after a couple of seconds of squeaking, sits up in bed and puts on the bedside lamp*) Beta. Beta. Beta?

SUKHESH: (*squeaking stops*) Yes, Ma?

MA: What are you doing?

SUKHESH: Hunting for bedbugs.

MA: Oh no! Again there are bedbugs?

SUKHESH: Terrible bedbugs!

MA: But where do they come from?

SUKHESH: Oh ... didn't you know? They are one of the side effects of getting married!

MA: That's something new! They were never there in my time!

SUKHESH: They must have been, or else –

MA: Or else what?

SUKHESH: I wouldn't be here.

MA: What do you mean? In this bed?

SUKHESH: On this earth. Bedbugs are crucial to the presence of humans on earth.

MA: And to think I never heard about this before tonight!

SUKHESH: Do you suppose you could put the light off, please?

MA: But I don't understand what the connection is between bedbugs and human existence!

SUKHESH: I can always explain tomorrow, Ma.

MA: (*peevishly*) That's what you say every night! But you never remember my questions in the day!

SUKHESH: That's because, between your questions and the bedbugs, I never get enough sleep! Now could you please turn the light off?

MA: Not until you explain about the bedbugs.

SUKHESH: Ma – be reasonable! I must sleep!

MA: Why can't you hunt for bedbugs during the day and answer my questions at night?

SUKHESH: I think the answer to that is obvious, Ma.

MA: Well, tell me anyway, damn you! You never talk to me anymore! Ever since you got married you've stopped talking to me!

SUKHESH: (*tiredly*) Okay. The reason that bedbugs can only be hunted at night is ... because we're in bed only at night. Pretty simple, isn't it! Now, will you put the light off?

MA: I don't think that's the right tone of voice in which to speak to your old, widowed mother.

SUKHESH: I didn't mean to be rude. It's just that I'd really like to get some sleep.

MA: Say sorry?

SUKHESH: (*helplessly*) Ma –

MA: Say it!

SUKHESH: Okay Ma, I'm sorry. Now –

MA: The least you can do is to be polite to the elderly. That's all we ask, a little politeness, a little respect –

SUKHESH: All right, Ma, all right. Now could you please turn the light off?

MA: (*reaching for the light switch, then drawing back at the last moment*) But what is the point, I don't know! The moment I switch the light off, you'll start hunting for bedbugs again – so where is the question of sleep?

SUKHESH: Ma, if you turn the light off, then I can hunt up a few bedbugs, and then I can get some sleep –

MA: A few bedbugs! How many are there, anyway!

SUKHESH: How can I know till I've had a chance to hunt them?

MA: You've had quite a few chances. After all, you got married just two days ago –

SUKHESH: (*bitterly*) And both nights you've kept me awake asking questions!

MA: And that reminds me – where is my daughter-in-law?

SUKHESH: Sleeping in the guest room, of course. Why do you ask?

MA: I can smell her hair in this room.

SUKHESH: Her hair?

MA: Yes. Haven't you noticed? Her hair smells like anything. It stinks! Phoo! Such a stink. I don't envy you your life ahead.

SUKHESH: I've never noticed any smell.

MA: It's right here in this room with us. Can't you smell it? Wahh! (*fanning her face*) It's choking me, it's giving me asthma! Are you sure she isn't in this room?

SUKHESH: Yes, Ma, I'm sure.

MA: But what about this smell?

SUKHESH: What kind of smell is it?

MA: Betrayal. The betrayal of mothers. The betrayal of mothers by sons. The smell of betrayal – and blood. Hot, wet blood! Aghhhh! The blood of a young woman, throbbing with redness and promise! Agghhhhhh! How I hate this smell! It's the smell of a woman in heat. (*turning suddenly towards him*) Is she hot, my daughter-in-law?

SUKHESH: How would I know? You've not allowed me to get close to her –

MA: (*fanning her face*) Ohhhh! This smell, this smell! It disgusts me, it blocks up my sinuses, it enters my veins and fills my uterus with pus! (*turning towards SUKHESH with a coy smile*) I still have one, you know!

SUKHESH: (*tiredly*) Have one what?

MA: Uterus! You haven't been paying attention to what I've been saying, have you!

SUKHESH: How can I pay attention, Ma, when I'm dizzy with sleep?

MA: Dizzy with bug lust you mean! Remember – before you can sleep, you'll have to hunt down all those bedbugs you mentioned!

SUKHESH: (*tired, resigned*) Yes, Ma.

MA: (*breezily*) Anyway, as I was saying, I still have my uterus! Many women my age don't, you know. Are you listening?

SUKHESH: (*tiredly*) What happens to them?

MA: They lose them to their daughters-in-law. At night, their daughters-in-law come creeping, creeping – and tear them out! And toss them up in the air! And suck them dry! Why do you think I told you never to bring my daughter-in-law into this bed with us? Because I want to keep my uterus! I don't want to risk losing it to that whore, that doll-faced pig, my daughter-in-law!

While she rants, furtively and then with increasing vigour, the squeaking of bed springs starts anew. But she is too absorbed in her diatribe to notice.

That's all that a daughter-in-law signifies - the loss of a mother's uterus, a mother's power! Once the daughter-in-law comes, the mother's life is over. Over! That's why the girl must sleep in the other room! That's why I must keep you, my sweet son, my only man, my lover, my joy, away from her! Away, away. Once a month you can go to her, of course. Just one day in the month. And during the daytime only.

The bed is by now jouncing along. MA is kneeling on the bed, addressing the audience, sometimes struggling to keep her balance as the bed sways and bucks.

And you can do what you have to do. After all, that's why you married her. To do that thing. And to get this house, of course. Without her, there would be no house. Or car, or TV, video - nothing. She's brought those things with her. I'll give her that credit. But she's also brought that other thing - that smell! That overpowering smell! I don't know how you will stand it, my son! My only son!

SUKHESH and the unseen AYESHA climax with hoarse cries and moans, subsiding gradually over the course of the next few lines. SUKHESH eventually flops over and lies back, panting.

I don't know how you'll bear to go into that room with her and do that thing that must be done - you'll have to run in and just quickly do it - just run in, push her down, force her legs apart and - once, twice, thrice - it's over. It's done. That's how it was with me. That was enough for me, wasn't it? And then I got you. All to myself. My little man. My son.

Finally she looks back and towards him. Her expression is full of love. She settles back under her sheets.

My darling son. (to the audience) See? He's fallen asleep at last. No bedbugs tonight. Oh no! I must see what I can do about those bedbugs. But not tonight.

The light beside the bed begins to dim.

Let him sleep. Tomorrow I'll do it. Spray the bed, perhaps. Leave the mattress out in the sun. Change the bed. And I'll do something about this smell as well. Get that indolent bitch, my daughter-in-law, to wash her head for once. Or cut it off? The hair, I mean, not the head. That would be expecting too much, wouldn't it? Yes, yes. Entirely too much. After all, they let me live, my mother-in-law and her son. But not much of a life. It's hardly been much of a life. Nothing in it, except for my son. My darling son, with his chubby feet and his tiny ... his tiny ... thing, like a small animal itself, a small fat hosepipe with a life of its own!

The light is now completely off. She is silhouetted against the moonlit window.

He never lets me look at it any more. Or touch it or hold it. Never. Not since he was twelve or thirteen.

And I'm so lonely, so lonely! I think I'll die of this loneliness! He never talks to me any more! He never looks at me any more! He never brings me presents or takes me out! Even to continue sleeping in his bed is so difficult! Me, his own true mother! Aahhh! Life is hard for mothers, hard, hard! I can't sleep for thinking about the hard places of life!

On an impulse she snaps the light on again. SUKHESH gives an involuntary grunt.

There! That's better. At least I can look at him, now. How sweetly he sleeps! I'll let him sleep now, shhhh! Sleep.

She turns the light off again.

Shhhhh. Sleep.

Gets under the sheet on her side of the bed.

Sleep. Sleep.

The moonlight in the window slowly fades out.

Curtain.

THE HUMAN REPRODUCTIONARY SYMPTOM

A classroom. There are three pupils and one teacher. The pupils, RADHA, NAFISA and JOSEPHINE, are in school uniform: white blouse, pleated skirt, tie. Preferably, at least one of these girls should be a man impersonating a woman. The girls are supposed to be around fourteen. Long plaits, hairbands, burgeoning breasts.

The teacher is addressed only as MISS. Her part is played by a man. She is tall, ungainly and is wearing a garish nylon sari. Her hair is scraped back in an untidy bun, she is wearing a large black tikka on her forehead and dark red lipstick. Her nails are painted scarlet, but are stubby. She bites them from time to time. She speaks in a high shriek.

Over the blackboard has been placed a huge, cheaply illustrated chart entitled, "The Human Reproductionary System". There are two figures on the chart, one man, one woman. They are shown standing facing forward with their faces turned to the side. The only feature which is unusual about this chart is that unlike others of its kind, in this one, the figures are fully clothed. Both are wearing Western clothes and their hair is blond. The chart is suitably labelled with a list of organs one might expect to see under the clothes of the models.

MISS: Girls, today we are going to study the human reproductory system.

(*assuming a sing-song tone*) The human reproductory system is a wondrous machine whose end product is further human beings.

Each and every one of us on Earth is the product of this machine.

This machine is composed of two parts. The male part and the female part.

Using her pointer, she indicates the two figures. When discussing the organs, she waves the pointers vaguely in the air in front of the chart, without looking over her shoulder.

The male part is composed of three organs. Nafisa! Take it down.

NAFISA has been staring fixedly at the chart rather than taking notes, unlike the others, who have been bent diligently over their notebooks, their tongues sticking out with the effort as they write.

The female part is also composed of three organs.

These three organs and the other three organs combine together to produce the Hormone Bearings.

Any quintals?

NAFISA: Miss? What are the names of the organs?

MISS: (*irritably*) I am coming to that! Have you understood this much?

NAFISA, JOSEPHINE, RADHA:

Yes, Miss!

MISS: (*resuming her sing-song voice*) The organs of the male are composed of two types. The Pipe organ. And the Test-match organs. There is one Pipe organ and two Test-match organs per male part.

The organs of the female part are also composed of two types of organs. The Eucharist and the Aviaries. There is one Eucharist and two Aviaries per female part.

RADHA's hand goes up.

Yes?

RADHA: Miss? What are the functions of these organs?

MISS: (*snarling*) I'm coming to that! Don't spoil my flow, stupid girl! Have you all understood this mulch?

NAFISA, JOSEPHINE, RADHA:

Yes, Miss!

MISS: All right.

The male part and the female part each to each have their wondrous specifications. Together they combine in the manufacture of the Hunger Bunting.

From the Test-matches of the male part comes the Semolina. The Semolina is composed of a billion trillion parts known as the Spare Matadors. Each Spare Matador is composed of one small head and one thrashing tail. (*MISS grows more animated and wherever possible accompanies her words with actions*)

JOSEPHINE: (*puts up her hand*) Miss, Miss! What does it mean, "thrashing"? What does the tail thrash?

MISS: (*throws a chalk at her*) Stupid girl! Pay extension! Am I not discarding everything in its wholesome enterprise? Just be still and give me your full ears.

So, I was saying. The Test-matches produce the Semolina. The Semolina passes down the Pipe organ and thence flows into the Eucharist.

Meanwhile, deep inside the Aviaries are a billion trillion Guava. These Guava are released one at a time. Unaided by human hand, the Guavum, once in a month, travels silky, silky, silky, until it entertains the Eucharist.

Meanwhile! Inside the Eucharist, the Semolina is waiting!

JOSEPHINE leans across to RADHA and whispers in her ear. MISS sees this.

MISS: Josephine! Stand up! Bad tiffin! What did you say!

JOSEPHINE: (*standing up*) Nothing, Miss ...

MISS: (*to RADHA*) Radha! Tell me, insanitary! What did she say?

RADHA: (*also standing up*) Miss, I don't know what she said!

MISS: What does it mean you don't know! Just repeat it out! If there is something to be exclaimed, let us all exclaim it!

RADHA: Miss, Josephine said, Miss, before the Semolina reaches the Eucharist, the man part must ... must ... Oh Miss! I can't say it!

MISS: (*murderously*) You just say it out, my girl, or I will come and regulate you!

RADHA: Miss, she said, the man part must put his Pipe organ right up into the Eucharist! (*she sticks her tongue out and covers her eyes with her hands*)

MISS: (*looking like thunder*) Josephine! Who has told you this nanosecond?

JOSEPHINE: (*looking repentant*) Miss, my brother, Miss.

MISS: What does your brother know? He is only a fool! Come here and I will spank your hands, naughty girl!

JOSEPHINE goes up to MISS taking her ruler with her, and stands meekly to receive two blows on each palm.

MISS: (*as she strikes JOSEPHINE's hands*) Nothing! Nothing! Wrong! Wrong!

Now go back to your seat and never let me hear you say robotic things again! As if the Pipe organ knows anything of the Eucharist! One is here and the other is there! What is the concoction?

NAFISA: (*putting up her hand*) But Miss? Then how does the Semolina reach the Eucharist?

MISS: (*as if this is obvious*) Through the Hyena, of course!

JOSEPHINE: Miss? What is the Hyena?

MISS: Uff! As if you don't know! Pumpernickel! Have you never exhumed yourself?

JOSEPHINE: (*looking deeply abashed*) No, Miss.

MISS: Silly crotch! Go to the bathroom at once and don't come back until you can give me a full rapport of your investiture! Go!

JOSEPHINE starts for the door, but stops and turns to MISS before she has taken two steps.

JOSEPHINE: But, Miss?

MISS: What is it now, you goosey bump?

JOSEPHINE: I don't know what to look for, or where!

MISS: (*appealing to the heavens for patience*) You don't know where to find your Hyena? Murder mysteries! What are we to do with geese like you? And I thought you were all Matric Pass!

NAFISA: (*putting up her hand*) Miss? I don't know either!

RADHA: (*hand up*) Nor I!

MISS: (*holding her head in exasperation*) This is the last stitch! How can I begin to postpartum the Human Petrochemical Syndrome if none of you can find your Hyenas?

(*to the audience*) This is what we reductionists have to face! Students who don't even know the biscuit pinnacles! And yet when they flay their exaltations, it is we who are blighted! Oh the ignition of it!

(*to JOSEPHINE*) All right! Get back to your seat, rictus! And all of you - for your homework tonight, half an hour in the bathroom, with a mermaid, inspect your Hyenas! And mind - only your own! Not anyone erstwhiles'!

Where was I? Oh yes. The Semolina in the Eucharist meets the solitary Guavum. The Semolina, you rekindle, is composed of a billion trillion Spare Matadors. Each Spare Matador has only one porpoise in mind and that is to infibulate the Guavum. Accordion, they all canter upon the Guavum until one and only one mangoes to pincer the mimosa of the Guavum. And thus contraption takes place.

Has everyone standardized?

NAFISA, JOSEPHINE, RADHA: Yes, Miss!

MISS: All right. Once contraption has taken placebo it is only a matter of months. The salads within the Guavum begin to masticate, to form the Ambrosia. The Ambrosia grows and grows and finally becomes the Footsie. Full nine months after contraption, the Footsie is purgated – and one more Ham Roll is burnished.

Is it clear?

NAFISA, JOSEPHINE, RADHA:

Yes, Miss!

MISS: Any catamarans?

NAFISA: (*putting up her hand*) Yes, Miss! I want to know, Miss – why do the male part and female part on the chart have yellow hair?

MISS: That is the breeding plumbago of the Hamadryad. (*responding to JOSEPHINE's raised hand*) Yes?

JOSEPHINE: Miss, why does the male part have covered legs while the female part doesn't?

MISS: For reasons of fission, only. Next?

(*responding to RADHA's raised hand*)

RADHA: Miss, may I go to the toilet?

MISS: Urticaria. And you needn't come backward – (*she looks at her watch*) It's already four throttle hive. What's happened to the cardigan?

Just then the school bell rings.

Ah! Vertigo! (*gathers up her things*) Oil rig, garments! Clique distress! Sea view snakes teak!

NAFISA, JOSEPHINE,
RADHA: (*together*) Goodbye, Miss!

Lights out. Curtain.

DOUBLE SOLITAIRE

A drawing room. In the middle of the room is a card table covered with a tablecloth. A man, ADIL, is standing by the window. He is dressed in an elegant, thoughtful way. He seems to be waiting. In his hands he has a new pack of cards with which he absent-mindedly plays, never looking at it.

The sound of a key turning in the lock of the front door. He turns, automatically putting the cards away in his pocket. A woman, ANAHITA, comes in. She is equally well dressed, in a clean-cut, unfussy way. She is chic without appearing to make the effort. They glance at one another, each smiling slightly, then she shuts the door.

He has not moved. She comes towards him. They do not touch.

ANAHITA: (*the expression on her face is that of someone suppressing a shared joke*) Well?

ADIL: (*he wears the same expression. He speaks softly*) You look lovely.

ANAHITA: (*her smile deepens*) So do you!

They share a smile. Wordlessly, he indicates the card table. They both approach it and sit down. There is something elaborate and ceremonial in their gestures. They face each other.

ADIL: (*cocking his head*) Shall we begin?

ANAHITA: (*reaching unhurriedly into her handbag, she draws out a matching pack of cards. She places it on the table*) I'm ready!

ADIL: (*drawing out his own pack*) And so am I!

If possible, a microphone is placed on the table to pick up the sound of the cellophane wrapper in great detail.

ANAHITA: (*seeming to pace herself according to a silent melody, she holds the pack of cards in her hands and with great, sensuous care begins to remove its cellophane wrapper.*) Don't you just ... love ... the way the cellophane slips off?

ADIL: (*he is watching her hands reverently*) Yes ... especially the way you do it. You make it seem so ... so ... effortless!

ANAHITA: (*softly*) There ... That's done. (*she looks to where his hands are still holding his pack in its pristine jacket*) Aren't you going to ... take yours off?

ADIL: (*as if just awakened to the fact that his pack is still wrapped*) Oh – yes! Of course!

ANAHITA: (*meanwhile, she is holding her pack up to her face with her eyes closed, lightly passing it back and forth over her mouth*) Mmmmm! New cards! I love to play with new cards. Smell them? They've been powdered! I can smell the powder even through the cover!

ADIL: (*slipping the pack briskly out of the cellophane and then smelling the cards, still in their cardboard container, perfunctorily*) Yes.

He seems slightly tense. He puts his pack down on the table and lightly turns it over and over between his hands.

ANAHITA: (*softly*) I'm going to take them out ... Ohh! Look it's sealed!

With infinite care, she breaks the seal on the cover. Then she prises up the folded "lid", runs her fingertip over each edge of the opened cover then taps the lower side of the container, quickly tips the cards out, preening as she does so.

MMMmmmmmmhhh. We should change our cards each time!

ADIL: (*smiling indulgently, as he opens his own pack*) Wait for me, darling – I haven't even got my pack opened yet!

ANAHITA: (*holding the newly opened cards fanned out against her face and purring as she smells them, runs the crisp, taut edges of the new cards against her lips and lightly nibbles the corners. Coyly, she discards the jokers*) Ohhh ... don't take too long over it! I can't wait to start ... shuffling!

ADIL: (*tips the cards out in one neat, tight bundle, catches them in his right hand and smartly taps the whole deck against the table's surface*) There! There we are! Come on! What are you waiting for?

They start to shuffle. She shuffles holding the entire stack in one hand, removing a few at a time from the middle with the other hand, places them on top of the stack and then resumes, a cyclical action that starts slowly but gradually speeds up. He, meanwhile, riffles the pack with manly vigour, making quite a racket as, with each riffle he realigns all the edges of the pack by tapping the table with them, then riffles out half the pack, transfers one half to each hand, taps again, then riffles the two together. Between the two shufflers, they build the momentum of their shuffling until they both stop, simultaneously, laughing and breathless.

ANAHITA: (*panting*) Oh – enough, enough! You always overdo the shuffling!

ADIL: (*smiling indulgently*) One can never overdo it! The cards have to be thoroughly mixed – now, come on –

They both start setting down their base pile as if running a race, each thumping down the thirteenth card, face up, with great panache, leaving it covered with their hands.

ADIL: There! You go first!

ANAHITA: (*throaty giggle*) No – you!

ADIL: (*taking the challenge*) Okay! (*lifts his hand*) It's a –

ANAHITA: (*she lifts her own hands simultaneously*) King! I go first! Yours is a ten!

Quickly she lays out her column and he does too.

ADIL: (*chiding her gently*) Uff! You're always so untidy!

He rearranges the cards so that each card in his column is neatly aligned with the cards in hers, there is a healthy space between both columns and the field itself is positioned symmetrically between the two of them.

There! You have to set them far apart enough, you know – so that the aces have place.

ANAHITA: (*amused*) Haha! Aren't we particular! Pull back the table cloth! Can't have any wrinkles getting in the way, can we? There! Now shall I start?

For the next couple of minutes the two of them play a very fast-paced game, concentrating so hard that the cards fairly fly from their hands ... they rise from their seats in the frenzy of play ... they slap down their cards with rhythmic coordination.

ANAHITA: (*crying out loudly, slapping down ADIL's hand, and laughing*) Stop! STOP! I can stop you - look?

ADIL: (*excitedly*) Nonsense! You can't stop me! That was a perfectly legitimate move -

ANAHITA: (*equally excitedly*) No, it wasn't! Look - you didn't see this one lying under here - take it back, take it back - see -

She moves some cards back, then starts to lay them out again, very fast. He smiles and concedes.

ADIL: Okay, okay - you're right - you go ahead.

He straightens up. They both sit down again. With a suppressed smile, she initiates play again.

ANAHITA: (*huskily*) Here ... and here ... and here ... and here ... !

ADIL: (*smiling sardonically down at the field*) I think ... you're going to win!

ANAHITA: (*sits back, arches her neck, takes a deep breath*) That's what you always say! And then at the last moment - (*she looks across with affectionate annoyance*) - you turn over three cards and they just fall into place like magic!

ADIL: (*playing a turn*) Now come on! Don't dawdle! It's your turn.

ANAHITA: (*inspecting the field slowly and carefully*) My turn, huh? Now let me see ... Not there ... not there ... (*she's checking to make sure that there aren't any cards to be built on to the ace suits*) not there ...

ADIL: (*mock impatience*) Hurry up, can't you? I can't wait all day!

ANAHITA: (*putting down cards*) Don't be impatient! I have to be sure ... Okay! There, there, there and there!

The phone rings, suddenly and raucously.

ANAHITA: Oh!

ADIL: (*annoyed*) Oh God! I hate being interrupted!

ANAHITA: (*pouting*) We should have taken it off the hook!

The phone goes on and on ringing.

ADIL: You get it. I'm not supposed to be home yet.

ANAHITA: No – you get it. If it's one of my friends I might get stuck.

ADIL: (*getting up quickly*) Oh, all right, all right!

His irritation is addressed to the telephone.

ADIL: I'm going to pick you up, can't you see? (*gets to the phone, picks it up*) Yes? Yes! Adil speaking ... yah, hi ... no ... I'm going to be in town tomorrow ... yes ... yes – listen? I can't talk just now, okay? No ... I'm, uh, busy. Okay? Yes – yes, we'll discuss it later! Okay! Okay – bye! (*puts the phone down*) Phew! He wanted to talk! (*takes the phone off the hook again, listens for the dial tone, puts the receiver down on the table*) I'm leaving it off the hook.

ANAHITA: (*during the phone call, she has been studying the field with great care*) I should hope so! Come quick! I've just thought of something exciting I can do in my turn –

ADIL: So do it!

ANAHITA: But it's your turn –

ADIL: (*studies the field briefly*) Oh, all right – how about this! (*he makes a few moves*)

ANAHITA: Ah! I was hoping you'd do that! Now you'll see!

ADIL: (*exclaims in delicious agony*) Oh – shit! I didn't see that!

ANAHITA: (*pausing in her tracks to give him the benefit of the doubt*) Is it all right? Shall I go on?

ADIL: (*in mock despair*) Yes, yes! Go on! You've got me now! You'll win, you'll win –

He only pretends to be covering his eyes as she quickly plays many cards on to the field. Suddenly he pounces and grabs her wrist.

Aha! I thought you'd miss that! STOP!

ANAHITA: (*squealing*) Oh no! Now you'll win! For sure! OHH! Ohh! (*watches him play a moment*) Oh wait! Stop, stop! Look at that one?

ADIL: (*playing spiritedly on*) No! You can't stop me now. There and there and –

ANAHITA: (*she leaps up and holds his hands, laughing all the time*) No! Stop! Stop! Stop!

ADIL: (*excitedly, getting up as well*) Look! If you move that one and that one –

ANAHITA: (*getting into the spirit of it*) Okay, and then? Oh! I see it – there.

They play out their cards simultaneously, laughing.

ADIL: No – no – put it there! Put it there!

ANAHITA: Look, look! It's going to work out – my cards are almost over – almost – almost –

ADIL: (*triumphant, slapping cards down wildly*) And – I'm – done!

ANAHITA: (*at the same instant, flashing down her cards*) Me too! Me too! Me too! WHOOOPS!

And they both collapse laughing.

ADIL: I won first!

ANAHITA: No – I did! I did!

ADIL: My cards went out first. Didn't you see my king?

ANAHITA: Pooh! Nothing without that queen there, from me!

ADIL: (*slumps back in his chair, slicks his hair back, smiling broadly*) Hmmph! That was fun! We really finished together this time!

ANAHITA: (*hugs herself and chortles a bit as she surveys the wreckage of the board*) Yes, we did! We really did! It really worked out completely!

ADIL: (*arching his back, stretching luxuriantly*) Mmmmmmmm! That was fun! An exciting game!

ANAHITA: Yah! Wasn't it?

ADIL: (*sitting back*) It's a great game!

ANAHITA: It is. I don't think I ever played it before meeting you –

ADIL: (*looks up amused and pleased*) Really? I taught it to you?

ANAHITA: (*leaning on the table*) Sure! Didn't you know?

ADIL: You never told me!

ANAHITA: Of course I did!

ADIL: But you play it so well!

ANAHITA: Well, it's ... very much like solitaire –

ADIL: Oh yeah – I know the one –

ANAHITA: Seven cards in a row, then six, then five.

ADIL: Yeah, I know what you mean – but this is better!

ANAHITA: Oh much! I never play solitaire any more.

As they talk, they gather up the cards. First they separate the two decks. Then they arrange each deck so that the pattern on the back is oriented the same way up. They do this as if they're quite used to it.

ADIL: Well, I must say. You're quite a professional!

ANAHITA: (*primly*) I've had a good teacher!

ADIL: Have you ever played with anyone else?

ANAHITA: Nah! No one I know would be worth playing with! Have you?

ADIL: Oh, a long time ago. But most women aren't really interested in it. I mean, maybe a game or two just to be polite, but that's all –

ANAHITA: (*smiling. She's completed her tidying up and is putting the cards away in their pack*) Well. I'm glad I learnt!

ADIL: (*he's finished too*) Yeah. (*puts his pack down*) So? That's it?

ANAHITA: (*she stretches*) Mmmmmm! Oh well. What's the time?

ADIL: (*looking at his watch*) Just three.

ANAHITA: That's all?

ADIL: (*sitting forward, looking wolfishly at her*) Yup! That's all!

ANAHITA: (*moves her head about, as if considering her options*) Look ... I don't have to be anywhere before five –

ADIL: (*starting to smile*) So?

ANAHITA: (*cocks her head on the side*) So ... I was just wondering ...

ADIL: (*leans his head on his hands*) And what were you wondering?

ANAHITA: Oh ... just ... (*she looks at him, her head to the side. She shrugs*) ... wondering ...

ADIL: (*roguishly*) ... Another game?

The lights start to dim.

ANAHITA: (*nodding her head exaggeratedly*) Yes! D'you think it's ... it's ... greedy to play twice in a row?

ADIL: (*smiling broadly and reaching for his pack again*) Sure, it's greedy! But so what? Let's be gluttons! Come on! I'll beat you this time!

ANAHITA: (*reaching for her cards*) Ohhhh! What fun! No! I'll beat you ...

Their voices fade out with the light. Curtain.

Introduction

The Rehearsal, The Wish, The Senses-Taker

These three monologues came into being separately. The reason I've grouped them together is because the theme of death touches each one.

The Senses-Taker came first. An interesting young actress got in touch with me sometime in 1997–98 with a request: would I write a performance piece for her? I call her interesting because of the odd combination of confidence and diffidence that she brought with her. She returned when I said I had something for her. She read the piece out aloud for me and we both agreed that it worked quite well. But that was the last I saw of her, which was a little sad. I had the feeling she was too idealistic to continue as an actress.

The Senses-Taker has not been performed in any form and I have rarely shared it with anyone. I am including it in this collection because, slight as it is, I continue to like it.

The Wish appeared several years later. *The Senses-Taker* had opened the door to short monologues for me. I'm not quite sure, but I think I wrote this partly in response to the 2001 declaration of India's one billionth citizen being born. The other part is that I am opposed to capital punishment. I'm always astonished at the vengefulness of otherwise placid, right-thinking friends, many of whom are ethical vegetarians. *The Wish* creates a somewhat unlikely connection between overpopulation and the extermination frenzy that overtakes otherwise reasonable people in the context of violent crime.

The Wish has been performed on stage a few times, sometimes in multiple voices (that is, not as a monologue). I've not attended any of the performances, so I don't have any direct experience of audience reaction. I've been told that there's often much negativity and pushback. The idea that capital punishment is morally repugnant is itself repugnant to those who consider themselves to be high-minded, moral and respectable. Those who feel strongly about the need to keep society safe from criminals, murderers, terrorists and others of that ilk are very sure that the remedy is to destroy the destroyers.

There are also, I am told, some audience members who find themselves moved and overcome or, at the very least, thoughtful.

In my view, the script has completed its task if it has caused audience members to question some of their beliefs. The work of actually changing minds and hearts is probably beyond the scope of an evening's entertainment.

The Rehearsal was initially titled "The Dancer" and then for a long time, "The Traveler". I was never quite happy with those titles and finally settled on this one in 2017.

The reason I wrote it was because my long-time friend and art patron Ranvir Shah was keen to connect me with another friend of his, the unique and exceptional dancer-performer Nirupama Nityanandan. Meeting her inspired me to write a piece for a dancer within the context of travellers, migration, translocation and their various interlinked shadows. The wished-for connection didn't result in a collaboration, but it left me with the monologue in hand. It's one of the few that I have personally read out loud, mostly to friends.

Odd fact: I tear up whenever I read it out loud. I don't know why. In early childhood between the years of six and eight, I learnt Bharatanatyam. I'm sure I had no aptitude, but I loved the costume, the make-up and the glittery hair ornaments. Maybe it's the memory of those distant, happy years that brings on the waterworks. Maybe it's the dancer's sublimation to something higher, something greater than herself. Maybe it's my fondness for that climactic moment at the end of a classic *alaripu* when the dancer's ankle bells produce a joyous clamour as she bends her head over her folded hands, honouring the audience and the Lord of Dance.

I once performed *The Rehearsal* as a two-voice reading with Kim Pereira, professor of theatre, Illinois State University in 2017. I was visiting for a week in connection with a student production of *Harvest*. Kim was an excellent co-reader and I greatly enjoyed the experience.

THE REHEARSAL

A woman traveller in her travel clothes with her carry-on baggage, standing in an immigration queue. The audio track plays airport sounds – announcements in the background and the rumbling murmur of 500 passengers trying to remain calm while waiting to pass through immigration. The audio track adjusts to the different demands of the story, as it proceeds. Some parts of the DANCER's narrative need to be performed as pre-recorded voice-overs.

DANCER: For ten hours we sit in the plane, live sardines in a dead tin. The crew changes, the plane changes, the time changes. Finally we take off. Two hours out of Madras there's an engine failure. We have a forced landing in Delhi. The crew changes. The time changes. The plane changes. We eat dinner at dawn. We take off again. We land again. This time we're diverted to Moscow, to Beijing, to Dubai. Our wine tastes of sweat. Our food tastes of snot. For dessert, we sleep. The crew changes, the airline changes. I forget the name of my destination. I forget my reason for travelling.

A never-ending tide of passengers encircles the globe. We fling ourselves upon cold inhospitable shores in successive waves, collect our luggage and vanish into the night. Grey desks, grey guards, grey lights. Announcements made in a metallic tongue.

Finally we arrive.

I stand in the queue, travel papers in my right hand, winter coat on my left arm, sling bag on my right shoulder, laptop carrier on my left, woollen scarf around my head. All around me the murmuring of lives in transit. I pick up stray threads of conversation, a word here, a sentence there. Not enough to stitch a full suit of meanings. I tell myself I need spectacles for my ears. Hearing aids for my eyes.

Then I am standing at the yellow line. Any moment now it will be my turn. Yes. Now.

I walk up to the counter. There's a man sitting behind it. I show him my papers. He glances at them. He glances at me. Then back at the papers. He asks, "What is the purpose of your visit?"

I open my mouth. I want to answer him. But no words come out. I have forgotten how to speak. I try to say the words, "I AM A DANCER!" But I left my words behind at the baggage claim counter in Singapore. I flushed them down the toilet in the aircraft. A fellow passenger stole them while I slept in the clouds but ...

As she speaks, she puts down her bags and removes her outer clothes. Her outer clothes are constructed to look like three separate pieces, whereas in fact they are one item with buttons in front. This single piece of clothing falls apart as easily as a dressing gown when its cord is undone. Beneath the outer clothes, she is dressed in a classical Bharatanatyam dance costume.

... wait! I am a dancer! I speak in more than one tongue.

I tell him:

(*she dances while speaking her lines*) *I ... am ... a ... dancer.*

He looks at me as if I have lost my mind. He says, "Madam ... I asked you a question! What is the purpose of your visit?"

I ... am ... a ... dancer, I say, in the language of the body.

He has never seen anyone behave like this. He says, "Madam, please! Excuse me! What are you doing?"

I ... am ... dancing ... at ... the ... feet ... of ... the ... Lord.

"Madam," he says, "if you don't answer me this instant, I will have to call airport security."

Listen ... to ... me ... listen ... with ... your ... eyes ... open ... and ... your ... heart ... unbound, I tell the man. *I ... am ... dancing ... at ... the ... feet ... of ... the ... Lord. He is Nataraja, Lord of the Dance, Nataraja the Untamed, the Unknowable. When he loosens his wild locks, Heaven itself sways to his command, the trees bend their crowns to Him and lightning flashes from His shining eyes.*

The man jumps up. He blows his whistle. Guards come swarming out of the walls, like termites. They grab me by my arms and drag me away. I am dazed and inert. I do not resist them. All the other passengers crane their necks in my direction, like chained dogs staring at the dog-catcher's van as it goes past. They are envious of me. At least I am no longer imprisoned in their queue.

The guards take me to a windowless room and leave me alone in there for a few minutes. A man comes in. He is older than the one behind the immigration counter. He wears a dark suit. "Madam, I am told you're not cooperating with our security systems," he says. "Please understand: we're not trying to harm you or to intimidate you. But we cannot afford to take chances. Even though you look harmless, you may be carrying a type of terror that we have not yet encountered. So please! Be considerate! Recognize that it's for the good of all travellers everywhere that we invent these procedures. Now then. Once again, what do you do and why have you travelled all this distance from your country to mine?"

I look deep into his eyes. I reach in with my entire being to strum directly upon the strings of his soul.

I ... am ... a ... dancer, I say while dancing. *I ... am ... dancing ... at ... the ... feet ... of ... the ... Lord. He ... is ... Nataraja ... Lord ... of ... the ... Dance.*

I stop. I see that the man is watching me with real attention. "I ... I think I understand!" he says. "You're telling me that you're ... a dancer! Isn't that right?"

My whole being lights up with pleasure! He understands me! I continue.

I ... am ... dancing ... at ... the ... feet ... of ... the ... Lord. He is Nataraja, Lord of Dance, the Untamed, the Unknowable. When he loosens his wild locks, Heaven itself sways to his command, the trees bend their crowns to him and lightning flashes from his shining eyes.

"Yes – yes – I hear what you're saying," says the man. "You are dancing at the feet of the ... the Lord – isn't that right? Have I got it? Good! Excellent. You're a genius – a divine spirit! Of course we'll let you in – we're not crude, primitive beings – in fact we'll give you a grant so that you can live here and teach some of us how to do that – how to dance at the feet of the Lord –"

Then he whisks me away and in time, everything he says comes true. I'm established at an excellent dance school, with my own group of students, with a grant and a permanent resident's permit. My voice returns to me and I can talk normally again, like other people. Time passes. Years pass. I am happy in my adoptive country and I settle down there. I fall in love with a man who understands my dancing and translates it for his countrymen. We marry and we have two children. My life feels complete.

Then one day I decide to travel back to the country of my origin. In all the time I've been away, I've not been back. I've talked on the phone to my parents, I've invited them to visit me, they've accepted my invitation twice, my sisters come often, on long holidays and one of them has spent a year studying at the university. But I myself have never gone back. When people ask me about it, I always say, "I don't know why. There's no reason. I'm not ready. I'm too busy. My children are small. My husband has sprained his right hand. My dog is expecting puppies. It's too cold here. It's too hot there. I am tired. I am busy."

The real reason though is that I'm frightened. I don't want to find that my country has changed into someone else's country in my absence. I don't want to find that I've changed into someone else in my absence.

Anyway, one day, I say goodbye to my husband and my children and I go.

The flight is pleasant and smooth, I travel business class and I am well rested by the time I arrive. I get into the queue for immigration. But when I am in front of the Indian immigration officer, once more I lose my voice. This time there's no reason for it. I am not tired, I am not afraid. The man looks at my foreign passport, he looks at my Indian face, then back at the passport. He says, "Madam, what is the purpose of your visit?" And when I open my mouth to say the words, no sound comes out.

This time I remember what happened on the earlier occasion, so I am confident of the outcome. I look at the man and say, in the language of dance ...

Once more, she begins to dance, as she speaks her lines.

Respected Sir: I am a dancer. I am returning to the land of my ancestors, to meet my parents, to honour the place of my birth, to watch the sun rise over the sea in front of my childhood home and to eat my mother's food ...

The man's eyes harden and his voice turns into steel bars. He says, "Madam! Behave yourself! This is an airport, not a dance hall! If you don't answer me properly I will call security –"

I open my mouth wide. I try to speak. But I already know it is useless. Once more, I begin to dance. *Sir ... please listen to me! I have only respect for you and your immigration desk! I want only to spend two weeks with my old parents, in the comfort of their home, enjoying the scent of my mother's kitchen –*

But the man's face has slammed shut. He calls the guards. I am hauled away. They throw me into a room without windows. I want to cry, I want to scream, but my throat's river has run dry and there's nothing I can do but wait.

After half an hour, a woman comes in. She is an official. Her sari is tense with authority. "What's this I hear?" she says to me, speaking sternly, as if to a child that has wet its bed. "What's this about dancing in the immigration hall?"

My eyes are full of tears. I still cannot speak.

Kind Madam, I say, *please open your heart, please listen to my message. I am just a travelling dancer, returning to my homeland. My parents are waiting for me in the arrival lounge. My children back at home are hoping to hear from me on the telephone to say that I arrived safely. My soul is parched with travel dust. Is it so hard to understand me? You who live in the land of Lord? You who hear the sound of his wild drum every day, you who sleep at his feet every night, you who live among the knotted locks of His boundless, eternal hair?*

I know that she hears me and understands me. Yet her eyes become like daggers and she stabs me with her gaze.

"Who told you to leave?" she hisses at me. "Who gave you permission to sell your flickering eyes, your graceful gestures and your sinuous neck movements in the vulgar Global Bazaar? Not I! And who is this Lord at whose feet you dance – is he the same one who uses me as his footstool? The one whose knotted locks cause power failures twice a day, whose boundless floods ravage my house every year, whose eternal shortages cause all the prices to rise – and yet I still light my lamp to him? Or is he the foreign Lord whose eagles will come screaming down upon my head if I try to detain you in my cell? The one who will have me sacked and my pension withheld if, by my actions, I crease your foreign forehead with a frown? The one with economic sanctions for his thunderbolt and dollars in his third eye?"

The fire of her speech melts my silence into ashes and burns open my throat. Words burst from my dam and I say, "You are right. I am a foreign citizen. And you have no right to hold me against my will. Let me go at once so that I can spend two weeks with the parents I left behind, in the home I had forgotten. Let me go watch the sunset that is hidden from me by the housing colony across the waterfront. Let me eat the fruit that's imported from China and bathe in water that's polluted with pesticides."

So she lets me go. And it seems to me that she smirks as I pass out of her power.

Two weeks go by. I go shopping in glittering malls, I draw money out of ATM machines, I eat cold pizzas out of damp cardboard boxes because my mother no longer cooks. And I cannot dance. Now I know why that woman officer at the airport was smirking. She knew that by allowing me to enter the land of my birth, she would succeed in silencing my ankle bells and strangling my feet.

After two weeks I return to my home across the seas. I get through the immigration formalities with ease. This time I can speak in words but my body is silent: I cannot dance.

I understand that everything I have done in my life so far has been a sham. There is no Lord, either here or anywhere else. Had I truly believed in him, I would find him wherever I lived or I would live wherever I could find him. Instead, I have lost him everywhere and found no-one else to take his place.

I give away my dog and I divorce my husband. I send my children away to their father's mother. I sell all my furniture. I go for long walks in the rain. I spend whole days sitting down in the middle of my empty apartment holding my feet in my hands, speaking to them. But they are silent and say nothing in return.

Existence ceases to have meaning for me. I decide to die.

She begins to mime her words.

So I oil my hair, I bathe in milk. I line my eyes with *kajal* and dress myself in bright clothes. I tie on my ankle bells and approach the boundary between life and death.

It looks just like an immigration desk. The Lord is sitting there, with his rubber stamp in his hand, his wild hair unleashed, his third eye flashing. When I approach the desk, he asks me in a voice like thunder, "Who are you, Madam? What is the purpose of your visit?"

I open my mouth to speak and of course ... no words come out.

But I am not dismayed. I have always known what to do at times like this. I have been doing it all my life.

She begins to dance.

Lord, I say to him. *I am one of your dancers. I have been dancing at your feet for the whole of my life, even though I have never seen you with my own eyes before. And sometimes I have doubted your existence. But here I am now! Take me into your country, Lord! Place your stamp in the passport of my fate!*

The Lord's face darkens and lightning slithers in and out of his streaming hair. "Answer me or I will call the security guards." Already they come running, the guards to the kingdom of the Lord. They look like ordinary people. They are my friends, my family, my lovers. "Answer me or I will have them drag you away!"

Lord! I cry to him, *You of all beings – to whom I dedicate my every breath, my every gesture – surely you know who I am – surely you understand the language of my dance – surely you hear the voice of my ankle bells?*

But the guards come for me anyway, and drag me back across the twilight lands and return me to the prison cell of my life.

This is where I am now, watched by all the guards. They are watching to see what I will do, now that my application to cross the border between the worlds has been rejected.

But it was only a temporary rejection, after all. That's what I have understood. At last, I am calm. Because I know that one day I will have all my papers in order. One day I will get the call.

She mimes her movements.

Till then, all I need to do is rehearse my answer. That's all. Rehearse, rehearse, rehearse. Keep rehearsing, never stop rehearsing. So that when the time comes I will get the answer right.

So I tie my ankle bells on tighter. I rearrange the flowers in my hair. I line my eyes with *kajal* afresh. I dip the tips of my fingers in red. And when people ask me what I'm doing, I tell them ...

Starts to dance.

I am dancing at the feet of the Lord ...

I am dancing at the feet of the Lord ...

I am dancing ...

I am dancing ...

I am dancing ...

I am dancing at the feet of the Lord!

She continues dancing until she reaches the end of the natural cycle of the piece, whereupon she stops as she would at the end of any performance and the lights snap off. Curtain.

THE WISH

A man stands alone under a spotlight. He is attractively middle-aged, urbane, well dressed. He looks towards the audience and talks in a friendly, conversational voice. He has something to lean against, ideally a bar while he half perches upon a bar stool, but a lectern will do as well. There is a large, bright red, cartoonish push-button switch in clear view, on the lectern/bar.

MAN: We had a visitor the other day, my wife and I. It was a Sunday and we were alone, no cook. It's an arrangement we like – gives us one day in the week when there's no one else in the house but us. (*smiles*) You know how it is. A little space to ourselves.

The doorbell rings. I answer it. There's a woman standing there, looking so gorgeous she literally drains light from the sky. Front, back, sideways (*mimes glory in face and form*) – *whoohoo!* She's wearing a slinky black outfit that shimmers in the gale force wind blowing in around her. I can hear the Sunday newspapers thrashing about in the room behind me, as I stand there with my tongue wrapped around my ankles.

She says, "Ah, thank you! May I come in?" Then she's inside and I don't remember if I stepped aside or whether she just walked through me.

I stammer, "D-do I ... know you?"

She flashes a blinding smile. "You do now!" she says.

My wife appears. She's wearing her Sunday caftan and her face is one big question mark.

"Hello!" says the woman, flashing a smile at my wife too. "Pleased to meet you! It's a great day to be alive, isn't it?"

My wife and I exchange glances. I say, "Uhhh ... sorry, but I – we ..."

She interrupts me, "You don't recognize me, right? That's okay – I didn't expect you to!" says the woman. "But the important question isn't who I am ..." she pauses dramatically, looking from my wife to me and back to my wife. "It's who *YOU* are." She looks expectantly at both of us, as if she's got this whole scene rehearsed and is waiting for us to respond to our cues. "Who *you* want to be. Today, tomorrow and for the rest of your lives ..."

I can hear my heart hammering – *whump-whump-whump* – like a diesel generator. With every pore of my skin I know there's something wrong with this woman. Something dangerous. I open my mouth –

But she stops me with one glance and says – "You're going to ask me to leave, aren't you? Yes! And you don't even know why! But I'll tell you why – because I can see into your head. It's because you're scared. Scared to confront your own deeper self – scared of your dreams – your fears –"

I raise my hands, and I'm not sure why I do that, it's like I'm defending myself. "Look – Miss – I don't know who you are or what you're selling, but we don't want it. Okay? It's a Sunday, and we like to be alone on Sundays –"

But she just laughs at me! She's got a wild laugh. Throws her head back. "Alone?! Hahahahaaaa! Hahahaha. Alone. Of course you want to be alone! And that's what I'm here to help you do. Make that alone-liness possible for you! Yesssss. I can arrange it for you – just for you! – if that's what you *really* want –"

My wife turns to me. "Who IS this?"

And the woman whips her head around in that serpentine way she has and says, "Thanks for asking, sweetie! I go by many names ..." She pauses like a model on the ramp, inviting us to complete her statement for her. But we don't.

"It doesn't matter who you are," says my wife. "My husband's told you to leave. I think you should leave."

"Oh my dears, my dears!" says the woman, "Don't you understand? The time for choices of THAT sort is over. There are *other* choices at your disposal – but we've not got around to talking about them yet, have we? No. We haven't."

She turns to me. "Your lives are about to change more fundamentally than you ever imagined possible and all you're thinking about at this moment is whether or not you're going to call the police."

I say, "Whatever. Please. Just ... go. Okay? Go!"

"No," says the woman. "Sorry, but I won't. I'm here for a purpose and I'll stay till I'm done and –" My wife's got her cell phone out but the mystery woman whips it out of my wife's hands quick as a flash – I literally don't see her move, she's that fast "– no phone calls either. Okay? Not till I say it's okay –"

"*Okay?*" says my wife, her voice sharp and angry. "What d'you mean okay – we're in our own home – *you're* the intruder –"

"The universe is a dangerous place, dearie," says the woman. "Believe me, I should know." Again she pauses, as if daring us to guess her identity. Then she looks straight at me and suddenly I feel the blood draining out of me, like water draining out of a bathtub. Every last ounce of heat and warmth vanishes with a gurgling sound that only I can hear, inside my head. I've looked into the woman's eyes and for the first time I notice that instead of pupils, she's got the whole universe in there – the starry blackness of deep space, complete with nebulae and spiral galaxies. Inside her eyes. I try to look away, but I can't.

"That's right," she says to me, in a matter-of-fact voice, "I may look human, but I'm not. I go by many names –" She stops herself. "But I'll spare you the list. For the moment, let's just say my name's ... Bonny. And I'm here to offer you a special, once-in-a-lifetime free wish."

"A *what*?" asks my wife. But I interrupt her. I tell her to look into the woman's eyes. "There's no point wasting time," I say. "We've probably got about three seconds before we'll have to make some unimaginable life-and-death decision – no multiple choice answers, no friends to call. We'll get one shot, and it's a lock, like it or not."

I've got to hand it to my wife – no doubts or denials – she's straight into attack. "I don't care who you are or what you are," she spits out at the woman or whatever she is. "I've never been a believer in hocus-pocus and I'm not going to start now! So you just take your wishes and leave this house this minute or I'll – I'll –" She runs out of steam. She's looked into the woman's eyes. She's smart enough to realize there's no point threatening a supernatural visitor.

"Excellent. You've both seen reason, and so quickly too! I like that," says Bonny in her purring, sex-nanny voice. "You can't get rid of me so we might as well play this game by my rules." She turns her head from one to the other of us, then decides on me. "You!" she says. "You've always wanted to do something for the world and all the people in it, haven't you? You've always believed you knew what the solution to the world's problems was. Well – now's your chance! I have an offer to make to you. A wonderful, magical, super-deluxe offer – it's right up your alley. It's what you've always talked about."

"Ummm ..." I say warily. "Meaning what?"

"Don't speak to her!" my wife says to me. "Tell her to stuff her filthy free wishes up her metaphysical bum and leave us alone!" But I shush her. The fact is, I'm curious now. I want to know what the offer is. You see, over the years, I *have* had a couple of ideas about how to improve this poor little planet on which we live. Well, only one, really. One big idea. And it's nothing profound or complicated. It's the kind of idea that most of us have had at some time or another, but we've never talked about it out loud.

Bonny knows, of course. "You're right," she says. "It's a common idea. Lots of people try it out in their heads. Some try it out in reality, but they're only human and they fail miserably. But I'm here today to offer you the chance to make it happen." Her eyes are digging into mine, like twin depth charges, delving down into the most hidden, buried reaches of my being. "Come on. Admit that you know what I'm talking about –"

"Not a clue," I say. But my voice is down to a whisper. "Pure moonshine and psychobabble –"

"Hah!" she says. "Liar! But okay, if you're going to be coy, I'll spell it out for you: you believe the world would be better off if a couple of billion people were to vanish from it, am I right? Well – AM I?"

She waits for me to nod. Mind you, I'm not proud about this, I know it's not nice, but – you want omelettes? You've got to break eggs. That's a simple, ordinary, everyday fact and I'm the kind of guy who's willing to face it. This world is overcrowded? We've got to remove people. "All right, then," says Bonny. "Now's your chance. I can help you make it happen –"

There's sweat trickling down the middle of my back. "What d'you mean?" I ask.

"I'm the ultimate people-remover. I can clear out whole cities. Whole continents. As easy as *this*!" She snaps her fingers. "Best of all, for today's special offer, I can do it with a minimum of pain and horror. Your victims won't suffer even a moment's premonition or anxiety. One moment they're here and the next moment – *zap!* – gone. Deceased.

Dematerialized. No mortal remains to clear up or dispose of, no mass graves, no funeral parlours. No mess, no fuss." She pauses. "So ... what d'you say?"

Out of thin air, she plucks a smooth round push-button and places it on the dining table – this thing here.

MAN indicates the switch-thing sitting on the lectern/bar. He picks it up to make it clear that it's not connected to any wires, it's an item all by itself.

She points to the button and says, "This button is how you'll do it. Think up a number and press the button. Immediately, that number of people will cease to exist – well, okay, not *immediately* but ... close enough. Plus, I'll stop time for you so you can do it calmly, without stress."

My wife's pulling at my arm, my mind's buzzing with static and in front of me, there's that button. I admit I am tempted. Overpopulation is the scourge of our times – who can deny it? Everywhere you look, there are hungry little mouths, clinging little hands ... an ever-increasing tide of tiny crawling bodies, with not enough air, water or land to keep them alive when they grow up. Every time you switch on the TV there's at least one shot of a starving mother, turning her hollow cheeks towards you, daring you to change the channel on her. And of course you do it – I do it – I change the channel on starving mothers all the time. But as I click away, I'm also thinking: wouldn't it be great if we could change the channel ... *FOREVER*?

There are names for people who think like me: *mass murderer; terrorist; monster* – arch-villains of our species. The worst of the worst. Yet ... look at me! I'm not a bad guy. I don't hate people! And I don't want anyone to suffer. But chiefly, I don't want *me* to suffer, I don't want my wife to turn into that starving mother on TV, I don't want my children appearing on the nine o'clock news covered in flies and blood. I want my children and my children's children – and everyone I know and care about and all their children – to live comfortably and happily forever and ever.

At the same time, I know it's not possible. There's not enough space, there's not enough time, and there's too many people.

So what's a man to do? Under typical circumstances, nothing. Send a few contributions to charity and change the channel until ...

Until there's a knock on the door and I'm offered a button to press, and a choice to make. A choice that'll make the world a safer, better place for everyone I know and love, and for all their children and for all the children yet to come. What should I do? What should any thinking person do?

I turn to Bonny and say, "No suffering? You're sure of that? What about all the grieving relatives, all the people left behind?" If I'm going to do this thing at all, I'm going to do it right. I'm not going to mess around. I'm going to eliminate four billion* people, minimum. Whatever it takes, whatever represents half the world's human population. And I'm going to be impartial. Men, women, children, the weak, the strong, the sick, the healthy – my chopping block will accommodate all, without distinctions of caste, creed or colour.

"Believe me," she says, and somehow, it's easy to believe someone who's got the universe stashed away inside her skull, "they'll blink out of the record, as neatly and completely as if they'd never existed. There will be no retribution, no enquiries, no consequences –"

My wife's tugging at my shirt behind me. She's wailing at me, "Are you crazy? There's GOT to be consequences!

* These numbers should be adjusted to reflect current statistics.

Have you thought about what's in it for her? Deals like this never come free!" My wife and I are not religious. We don't go to any churches, temples or mosques. We don't believe in immortal souls or after-lives or before-lives. Yet I know exactly what she's thinking. The only time we've ever come across deals like this, it's been in books and stories. And in those books and stories, the person handing out the registration forms is called the Devil.

Sharp as a pin, Bonny turns to my wife and says, "Sweetie, ordinarily? You'd be right to be concerned. Souls are lost, reputations are ruined, operas get written. But this time, as it happens, it's a genuine, no-strings policy. There are no forfeits. No hidden clauses."

My wife's voice is low now and her eyes are frightened. "Who *are* you?" she asks again. "What is your name?" But the time for answers is over.

I turn to Bonny and say, "Look. I'm going to accept your offer. Actually, you probably knew that all along, so this silly charade of me making a choice is just that, right? A charade. So let's get on with it. You said I had to name a number and –"

Bonny's smile is gentle this time, it has less teeth in it. She says, "All right, listen up – but don't worry, I can always repeat myself. Time is no longer an issue. If you feel confused, you can stop to ask me questions and I will explain whatever needs explaining, as patiently and slowly as you might need.

"You decide how many people you want to remove. If you want to specify male or female, age or ability, specific human communities, religious groups or racial types – you can do it. Just say out loud what your choice is. Then when you're ready to begin, press the button. A face will appear to you, of a victim. If you press the button again, that person will dematerialize and your next victim will appear. And so on.

"Remember, time has stopped for you: you will feel no fatigue, no loss of attention. Each successive victim will seem as fresh to you as the very first one – and that'll go on and on, for however many victims you choose, until you've eliminated the number you set out to eliminate. After that you'll be returned to normal time, with no ill effects and no reprisals. The only rule is that once you terminate someone, he or she can't be brought back to life. What's dead is dead."

My wife's pleading fades into the background. I turn to face the button. "I'm ready to begin," I say. "I wish to terminate one half of the world's current population, whatever it is. I will not discriminate against any racial or physical type. I would like the widest possible geographical mix of people, selected randomly." Then I look at Bonny and she nods to me, telling me to press the button.

MAN mimes his own actions as he describes them. A slide show begins as he talks and the images match whatever he says.

The moment I do that, a face appears to me. It's a woman's face, a young woman. Around seventeen. Her face is blown up huge, so that I can see every pore of her warm, brown skin, every eyelash, every grain of her wide, dark eyes. She can't see me, but I can see her and not only that, I can hear her thoughts – no, more than that: my mind is merged with her mind. So, yes, she's seventeen, she's on the brink of college, she's got a boyfriend whom she loves and another one whom she merely flirts with – and, well, you get the picture: all her thoughts, memories, emotions and ideas, wants, hurts and fears are made known to me in a single instant. Meanwhile, I retain awareness of my own thoughts and memories.

Frankly – (*slight chuckle*) I mean – there's no question about it: I can't just cancel out this young person's life! She's ... oh, come on! She's cute, she's a girl, she ... doesn't fit the profile. I look at Bonny. Bonny looks back at me. "What's the matter?" she asks.

"For my first victim," I say, "I think I ... well, I'd rather have a more ... *generic* person."

"There are no generic people," says Bonny. "Every person is specific. But never mind: if you have an image in your mind of a *generic* person, this is the time to spell it out. Go on – just do it. This is your show. No one's going to criticize you or make you eat your words. Describe to us what you mean –"

So I give it a try. "All right, I'd like the first person to be a man. A middle-aged man – I guess someone a bit like me but – okay, not ... you know ... maybe not Indian because I don't want any of my friends or relatives to show up – but Asian, any kind of Asian – well, all right, let's just say a brown-skinned man, middle-aged, medium height –"

"Press the button," says Bonny. So I press it.

Immediately, he appears. A middle-aged man, his face blown up huge. He looks roughly Middle Eastern. As before, his eyes are open and my mind is merged with his and I retain awareness of my own thoughts and memories.

I realize that he has a wife, three children and an ailing mother – I know every detail of his life. What takes my breath away is that the ordinariness of this life is, simultaneously, the most extraordinary thing about it. The details are different but – give or take a few sisters, nephews-in-law and second cousins – he could be me! He *is* me – except he's a stranger whom I'll never meet.

I feel a disturbance deep within me. I do not want this man to die.

Once again, I glance at Bonny. Perhaps there's a frown on my forehead. "All right, I'll pass on this guy too," I say. "He's ... well, he's in the midstream of his life, he's healthy, he's happy, he's ... just ..." I shrug. "He's an ordinary guy and it's not his time yet."

Bonny says, "That's okay. No rush – take as long as you wish. You won't age or lose points or anything. Maybe the trick lies in being *more* specific? Don't be afraid! You're saving the planet! Think about the kind of person you'd *like* to cancel out of existence."

"You're right. Maybe I've not got the hang of it yet," I say. "How about this: a man again, this time a young punk, a real low-life. He's a drug peddler and a pimp ..."

My mind fills again. This time I see a firm young face, male. He has slanted eyes, and full, thick eyebrows. His head is shaved and he has a tattoo on his left cheek, of a scorpion. For an instant, I am disgusted by him – then his thoughts become my thoughts. Fear is his constant companion – and it becomes my constant companion too. Hunger gnaws at his gut and at my gut too. The pain of frequent failures, the exhilaration of defeating a street rival, the sweetness of a honeydew melon – all these and much more pass into my possession.

Yes, he raped his sister, as a result of which she ran away from home, became a foul-mouthed slut and died before her twelfth birthday. But the punk's elder brother is a saint: he's the family's breadwinner, works as a shop assistant by day and runs a roadside stall at night. The punk loves him – hey, the punk feels love! Who would've thought it? He adores his elder brother and dreams one day of being like him, legitimate and clean, a pillar of society. The father of the family vanished years ago. The mother is dying of cancer and there's no one to care for her except the punk. Every morning, every evening, before going out to deal his drugs, he washes her with his bare hands and lights candles for her in church.

The young man's skin is peach-brown and hairless, his face is so taut and fresh it's almost edible. Yes, his life so far has been, and still is, brutish – but it is also unbearably tragic. He is just sixteen. There are tears stinging my eyes.

"Not him either," I mutter.

Bonny says, "Maybe you should try random selection again? I think your notion of villains isn't working out the way you thought it would ..."

If slides are used, the selection now flicks by with only brief pauses, showing the widest possible variations on the human type.

Briefly, I return to random selection. I get sweet-faced nurses and rheumy-eyed grandmothers, god-fearing Irish dockworkers and ancient Botswana farmers tilling their fields under the blazing sun. I turn to Bonny and say, "It's not working. I can't manage with this kind of selection! I need to find people who I ... I ... don't *mind* dispatching!" She nods understandingly and tells me to keep trying.

So I go back to certified bad guys: gunrunners, mobsters, cold-blooded torturers – torturers! Can you believe this? You'd think a torturer would be impossible to sympathize with! But no, it makes no difference. I get a pale, thin-faced man, East European, perhaps. I look into his eyes, I see what he sees and pain convulses me like a dozen tidal waves at once. The pain of ultimate horror, of degradation and self-hate. The torment of being despicable on command, of tearing out nails for a living, of becoming the stuff of nightmares, of clinging to tiny shreds of decency, then losing them to the stench of body fluids, to screams, to curses. Day after day. The torturer sits in his den of suffering, clutching his own child's picture to his heart, savouring memories – a golden summer's day, the taste of his wife's cooking, the sound of a mandolin.

"Not him," I whisper, "not him." My eyes are damp – for a torturer! Ahh – I hate myself, I curse my sentimentality. I'm trying to save the world and here I am sympathizing with worthless scum!

I trawl the lower depths of humanity. I ask for hired assassins and prostitutes, serial rapists and suicide bombers. I ask for arms dealers and filthy politicians, I ask for pimps and flesh peddlers, caste murderers and drug lords – but each time, every time, the story is the same: the moment I can hear their thoughts, I cannot push the button.

I try to go lower down the scale. I ask for a sociopath, a man who works as a paid assassin and kills for pleasure. I get a guy with a face like an angel and an inner life so heady it's like a multicoloured carnival – he's a human firework, forever bursting, forever glorious. Yes, he has no moral compass – yes, he's without remorse and feels no pain or sympathy for anyone – but oh, the serenity he knows! He performs like an artist, with clarity and even a certain crazed kindliness: he believes he's the angel of death, doing God's work. He believes he is kinder and more compassionate than the surgeons who use scalpels to torment the lives of those too ill to protect themselves. Unlike cancer or old age, the death he provides is quick and painless. He smiles in his sleep.

I tiptoe away from him, shaken, awestruck.

I ask for a drug-crazed whore – hoping to find someone so degenerate that I'll be able to dispose of her happily, as a favour to her. I ask that she be grotesquely ugly so that my task is not compromised by pity. Believe me, I am growing desperate. I want so much to begin my purge of humanity! I am sent a woman who is bald and pock-marked, covered with tattoos and infested with every form of venereal disease known to humankind. My hand hovers over the button, ready to plunge but ... when my mind merges with hers, I discover that she lives only for her daughter, a sweet-faced innocent ten-year-old girl who lives with a neighbour, goes to school and thinks her mother died in childbirth. The whore paints her face, wears her wigs, turns twenty tricks a night, is routinely locked up and raped by policemen only so that by day she can sit in the street corner and catch a glimpse of her child playing in the park.

My eyes are streaming. I pass.

I ask now for a serial rapist, a desperate, angry, filthy being. Someone who destroys the lives of women remorselessly, someone whom I can feel righteous about dispatching. But even as I form my description, the doubts begin. Sure enough: I get a mean, hungry predator, a man with a keen, fierce knowledge of where and when and how to strike. He lives at the knife edge of extreme desire, always searching, always frantic. His fire is lit by another person's screams, so – yes – he is despicable ... as despicable as anyone who places his own desires ahead of anyone else's – his own desire for omelettes ahead of someone else's eggs. Like the imperialist who steals from one country to make his own country rich. Like the mother who starves her daughters so that her son can eat. Like the religious leader who burns down mosques or temples so that his mosque or temple can be built.

Like me, for placing my ideas for a better life ahead of the lives of *four billion* others ...

So, yes. I crawl away from the serial rapist, appalled and humbled.

And so it is, so it is – with *every type of person* I pull up. Good or bad, when I can look directly into their eyes, and think their thoughts, breathe their breath, I cannot pull the plug on their lives. Child molesters and terrorists, smugglers and bandits, carjackers and sex traffickers – once I'm inside their heads, the heat of their lives is like a volcano of sensation – even for the brain-dead! The mentally deficient! The depraved and the suicidal!

The anorexic girl who eats half an apple a month, who looks like the walking dead, who lives only for that moment when someone will nourish her with love, not food! The autistic boy who lives in a world of beautiful abstractions, marred by the continuous distraction of those whom we call normal! The old lady with Alzheimer's, so deficient in brain activity that all she can produce, when I encounter her, is a sad, simple twittering: *I am, I am, I am. I ... I ... I ... Am.*

For all, for everyone, that hypnotic song: *I am, I am, I am.* The force of life within each living being is a torrent, a tornado, a furnace that burns so fiercely that I am cooked to a crisp from the first moment of contact.

My eyes are streaming – I am dazzled, I am undone. It's not that I feel sorry for each person I encounter. It's that I realize in a way I never understood before, the terrifying sweetness of being alive.

For kings and lepers, saints and fiends – it makes no difference: the sweetness is the same. And that's terrifying, isn't it? To know that every single breath is more precious to the mouth to which it belongs, than a thousand mountains made of gold. That for all our separate vanities and ambitions, all our colours and convictions, we are threaded along a single strand of air, like beads along a necklace that is *eight billion people* long.

And I could not snip a single bead away from its fellows without destroying the entire necklace. Not a single one.

You would think that I would grow bored or de-sensitized or jaded – but of course, I do not. As Bonny told me from the start, I am living outside of time. So there's no sensory overload, no numbing down, no fatigue. Every person is the first person. Every story is the best story. Every life is unique.

I feel so *outraged*! If only I could press that stupid button without having to experience each separate life before I snuff it out! If only I had faceless, anonymous numbers to deal with! I turn to Bonny and I *beg* her to let me just state my number and press my button. That way, I can succeed in my mission, which is humanitarian, after all, it's for everyone's benefit, if only I could *Just Do It*. But she shakes her head and tells me what I already know: there's only one way she'll let me do it and that's her way.

I don't give up easily. I persevere through hundreds of would-be victims. But in the end I turn to Bonny in defeat. "I can't go on," I admit. "I want to end this stupid experiment, this simulation, this booby-trapped wish! Without detachment, how can I perform?" My eyes are streaming freely. I have no idea whether I'm crying for myself or for the planet or for all the individual lives whose stories have left me raw.

This cruel travesty of a wish – offering me the chance to save the world, while showing me that I'm so weak and sentimental I can't terminate even one person, never mind four billion. Who *IS* this Bonny? I find myself wanting desperately to know.

My wife is standing beside me. She is quiet too and has tucked her hand into mine. Her face is wet. We are both trembling. I don't know yet what she's understood of my experience, but I suspect she saw whatever I saw.

The slide show ends with a slow fade-out – perhaps it is a montage of all the faces that have appeared.

Bonny asks me if I'm sure I want to stop. I tell her I am. We return to normal time and the newspapers which had been silent for the duration of the ordeal begin to flap and flutter once more in the breeze caused by Bonny's presence.

I ask Bonny point-blank: "I have to understand this – are you the Devil? Or are you God?" I realize, as I ask this, that the question belongs to the moral science classrooms of my childhood. I never expected to need it at any time in my adult life. I feel embarrassed asking it.

She shrugs, saying, "Neither and both. Whichever name you give me, it is not my true name."

I ask her, "What happens next? What have we achieved?" I was thinking about the planet. About my failure to improve anything. About the hungry mothers, the dying children, the lack of space.

"You tell me," she says, with a slight smile, "I'm always listening." There's a finality in her voice and I can see the ends of her hair fading from sight. The wind that brought her in is starting to blow the other way. "I can show you the water, but I can't drink it for you."

My wife says, "Wait – please – may I ask a question?"

Bonny says, "Sure, go ahead –" She's fading fast but her voice is still crystal clear.

"I want to know why you chose us – I mean him, my husband – is there a reason?" Neither of us thinks this question is insulting to me. If she hadn't asked it, I would have. "You had eight billion people to choose from, so ... why *him*?"

And Bonny says, "Why not?"

Lights snap off. Curtain.

THE SENSES-TAKER

A woman of indeterminate age answers the knock on her door.

WOMAN: Hello? Yes? The what? The ... senses-taker? Senses? (*she looks bewildered*) But ... I ... (*shrugs*) I've never heard of such a thing! Is it possible? (*looks quizzically at the visitor*) After all ... how do you do it? (*pause*) Fill up a form, eh? Just like that? And for all the senses? (*laughs*)

Huh! Doesn't make "sense" to me!

(*listens attentively*) Okay ... okay ... (*a cunning expression appears on her face*) Just a minute! Free, did you say? You're relieving me of some senses - and you're doing it for free? (*laughs now, more heartily*) Why, now! If that isn't the funniest thing I've heard! Hawhaw! Something for nothing! (*stands aside to let someone in. We never see this person or hear his/her voice*)

Most often, when people knock on my door it's either to sell something or to buy something. Either way, there's no freedom! But you? You offer me nothing for something and then you ask for a gift! That's what I call rich! No one's ever asked for a gift from me.

Better sit down in that seat - quickly, before I find some way of charging you for it! (*laughs again*) As you can see, I have a grand choice of seats! Yes. A grand choice - exactly one!

She settles herself on the floor. There is a space between herself and her guest.

Now then. (*she leans over to look at the form that is being offered to her*) So this is the form? (*she strains to read it*) Well, well. My eyes aren't so good any more. (*she holds the paper this way and that. From the way she holds it, it's obvious that she's illiterate. Finally she gives the form back to her guest*) Tell you what. You look like an intelligent person! Why don't you read this out to me? Then we can proceed.

Right! *Ahem*! Name? Name! Well 'course I have a name! Everyone has a name. Even my cat there has a name – and it isn't even human! So what's my name? Well, well, let's just say it's ... Hero. That's right. Hero. What? You don't think it's a real name? But it is! The only name I've ever had. How did I get it? (*shrugs*) I don't know. You'd have to ask my mother – except you can't. Not alive. Not been alive for a long time. I can't really say how long. As long as I can remember.

What's that? My *father*'s name? And supposing I don't have a father? What? Naaah! That's not true! Lots of people don't have fathers! You've just never met any of them – that doesn't mean they don't exist! No fathers. I'm sorry – but that's the truth! I can't help it if your form demands a father's name! Coz I can tell you, I've never heard of anything remotely like a father in my life. And I've lived a long time. A long time.

Of course, other people have fathers. But not me. No. My mother and me, that's all. I had no father because no father would have me. For him, I didn't exist. So for me, he didn't either.

(*pause, while she listens*) No, of course I didn't miss him! You've got to have things before you can miss them! Look at me! I've never missed anything in my life. Coz I've never had anything.

No ... no, my mother died shortly after I was born. All she left me was my name. So I didn't really have her either. Oh, I've had aunties, of course. Lots of aunties. But aunties don't belong to anybody and nobody belongs to them. aunties and uncles – sure, any number. And I shared their things and they shared my things – but that's not the same as having my own.

Yes, okay.

You've got a point there. I have my life. But then again (*laughs*) it's not something I can miss, is it? Either it's there or – it's not! And then I'm not, either.

(*she relaxes somewhat*) I must say, your form is full of the strangest things. Why don't we leave this issue of names and get on to something more interesting?

Date of birth – oh, that's easy. It's the first of the year. What? Oh, every year of course! Huh? What d'you mean, year of birth? No, how should I know? I was a baby then! Babies don't remember such things. Look, it's not my fault if your form is full of pointless questions! It's not as if I asked you to let me give you answers, you know! Yes, yes, write whatever you wish. Forty or fifty or even sixty – what does it matter? It's not as if a life can be extended or shortened by the answers given in forms!

What will you know from the date? The date of birth is nothing. The length of any person's life can be known by dividing the height of their mornings by the depth of their nights! What else? For some people it is more and for others it is less – regardless of their date of birth. Who can say whether your eighty years are more than my five? Or my five minutes less than your ten years?

If you ask me to tell you what I think my age is, I'd say about two hundred and seven! Yes! The seven is for when I was a child.

All children grow to be seven years old, not just me. In each year of childhood something special happens.

In the first year you learn to eat and shit. In the second year you learn to walk. In the third year you learn to talk. In the fourth year you learn about death. In the fifth year you learn to take care of other children. In the sixth year you learn about money. And in the seventh year you grow up.

Of course it happens suddenly! One day you're a child and the next day, you're not. With me it happened late in my seventh year. I was already at my full height. Hair was starting to sprout in new places every day. Sooner or later, someone noticed the hair. And brought my childhood to an end.

There's a knocking at the door.

Will you excuse me? I need to do a little work now. It won't take long. Will you still be here when I come back? It'll take five minutes. Just wait. Okay. Thank you.

She goes "out", remaining out of sight for a few moments, then returns. She looks tired. This might be achieved with dimming lights or by physical movement.

You're still here, I see! So? How much longer do you think this will take? No ... it's just that people ask, you know. They like to know what's going on in here. They say they don't believe anyone can be interested in taking another person's senses. They say that sounds like non-sense (*laughs at her little joke*). Huh! Sometimes I think I'm growing too old for this work. It tires a person out. (*smiles*)

Yes. I was wondering when you were going to get around to asking me that. My work. Well, that's easy too. I do relief work. People come to me and I take their burdens from them. All kinds of burdens.

They pay me for it, of course, but only for a small part of it. The larger part can't be paid for because the larger part isn't visible. I'm paid only for what's visible. And that's just a teaspoon of stuff. Just some stuff – no importance in itself. But if a man keeps it stored up inside him, he begins to weaken. So he has to get rid of it. That's what I do. Help him get rid of it. Mind you, it takes a struggle! You'd think they'd be keen to give it up, their little teaspoon! But no, it has to be coaxed out of them, like milk from a dry cow. And that's just the visible part. The invisible part leaves a man in a great heaving rush – *hoosh*! All the tensions that have collected over the course of a day or a week.

(*laughs*) What a struggle we have sometimes, my! Some men give a great bellow when they let it out. Other men are silent. But usually, the strangest thing is, they are not grateful. They hate me for relieving them of all their stored tensions! So they pay me for the little teaspoon which is the visible part and they don't even mention the other portion. The part that I can see and feel but never talk about.

(*pause, as she listens*) Women? Yes, women have tensions too. And they carry them around just like the men do, bent over like coolies at the station with the weight. And yes, I relieve those burdens too, sometimes! Women's burdens. But – heh! (*a dry laugh, which degenerates into a cough*) you know what? They don't pay at all! They feel so guilty to be relieved of their burdens that they come to me only when they're drunk or sick. And they never admit to anyone that they have been with me. And the only women who come are others in this place where I live, others whose task in life is to relieve burdens –

There is another knock and she excuses herself again and returns as before, exhausted. A little more this time. Her breathing is uneven, her movements slow and laboured. She seems to have aged since the time she left the room.

I'm not sure how much longer this can go on, you know. They're beginning to wonder, the people outside. They're wondering why you want to spend so much time here. They don't believe anyone can be so interested in my senses. You better finish up soon. (*pause*) I don't feel too bright either. It takes a lot out of me, talking. I don't usually talk so much. (*coughs*) Don't get the time. This kind of work – it's never-ending. There's no end to the burdens that need to be relieved.

(*coughs*) But go on, go on. Ask me your questions. Might as well finish it, now that you've begun. I couldn't refuse you even if I wanted to – that's the truth, isn't it? Yes. I had begun to suspect it a little while back. Never mind. I don't hold it against you. After all, that's what my whole life has been, to be the answer to other people's questions. Not the right answer, not the best answer, but an answer nevertheless. So ask me, ask me.

(*tired laugh*) Or ... never mind. I know what the next one is. It always comes up, one way or another.

Male or female?

Huh! I am whatever you want me to be. But I am the answer, not the question. I am the answer to all types of questions.

I can answer with three mouths, I can speak with two tongues. But I can ask no questions. What more can I tell you? (*shakes her head*) I am what I am. I can't change myself to suit your form.

Next question! (*coughs*) Okay. Yes, I have children now and then. They come out incomplete – like half finished dreams. People around here tell me that's the most I can have. So I have a cat instead.

(*indicates the cat, calls to it. It approaches and climbs into her lap*) See? This is my only child. (*pets the cat*) There, there! I call him Sona. (*laughs*) No! He's my cat, but he doesn't belong to me. He belongs to himself – see? (*the cat walks off*) He's had his fill of me and now he's gone again. He's just another questioner in the end!

Better ask me your next question. (*she seems to be weakening. Coughs weakly, intermittently*) I don't know how long I can keep answering.

(*listens*) Now. That's a difficult one. Religion. I don't know. On the one hand, I'm ready to believe in anything. On the other hand ... how can I believe in something when nothing believes in me?

Look at your form – even your form does not believe in me! It asks me questions that I cannot answer – about names, for instance, and fathers!

(*coughs*) In all the gods there is only one in whose face I can look and find some reflection of myself. But even he ... is a he! Whereas I, I don't have words that properly belong to me: I am not she, I am not he. Nevertheless I exist. Even though I have no words for myself, you have come here to count me too, haven't you? And that's proof, isn't it? That I exist?

Even though no one else around here admits that they can see you! They tell me that I'm talking to myself. That's why they keep trying to pull me out of this room, to squeeze some more work out of me. Coz they don't believe that I can have a senses-taker. That I can be counted.

There is a knocking at the door.

See? You hear that? (*shouts to the door, weakly, though*) I'm busy now! Leave me alone! I need rest!

Further knocking.

Tell them Hero's tired! Tell them Hero's asleep for once! Yes! It's too late, it's too much! Leave me alone!

(*She looks towards the door, then turns to her guest*) Yes. Where was I? Religion.

(*coughs and in the effort of coughing finds herself lying down*) Ah, excuse me, excuse me. I need to lie down. I feel the need to lie down. You can go on asking me questions, though. It's all right. That's what I'm here for, to answer questions. And that's what you're here for too, isn't it? To take my answers, to count my senses up. Yes.

She turns with difficulty from her side to her back, breathing hard.

So take them then.

Which sense do you want to take first? Come on, then, come on! Don't be shy! All right, make it my eyes. My eyes are yours to take.

The stage lights begin to dim.

Okay, next! Is it smell? Yes, take my smell! And next it'll be the ears – because I can hear you without them, in my lungs and in my pulse – yes!

(*her panting breath is strangely erotic*) The ears have gone! And the skin too – and I am now limitless! Released from the prison of dry wrinkles! I know you only by the taste of you in each of my three mouths, and both my tongues and ...

(*her belly heaves up from the floor, as if drawn up of its own volition*) now ... now they too are going ...

(*from the region of her navel, there is an intense glow*) have gone ...

(*the stage is in darkness. Only one light remains, the navel light*) ... have gone, and – what's this, what's this? I have lost all my senses, but one yet remains ...

There's a burning, burning, burning in my belly! What's this that I've never noticed before? The sense of being in a body!

(*only one point of light remains, the navel light, which moves up and down, with the distinct rhythm of a pulse*) A bright sense, a lighted sense! Ah! Senses-taker! AAH! (*the navel light begins to fade, dying quickly*) you *have* relieved me, after all!

All lights go out.

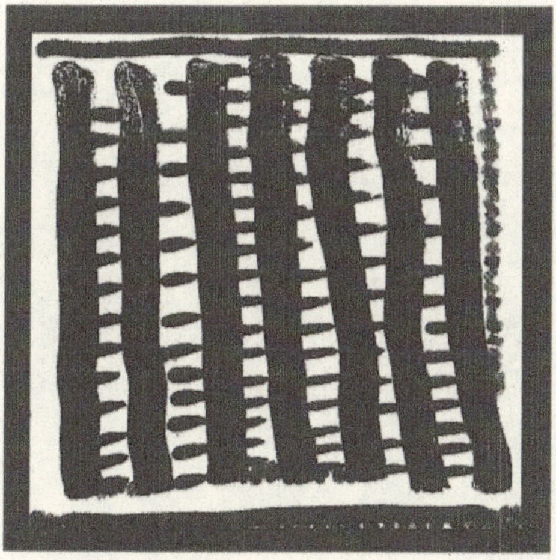

Introduction

Hidden Fires

These five short monologues were inspired by political events in India. However, even as I wrote them, the thought occurred to me that it might not be very smart to link them to specific people or incidents. I am not especially brave. I do not align myself with political parties or associations. The closest I come to belonging to any group is by avoidance: I belong to that group whose members don't belong to any group.

There are no places, dates, political issues or ideologies named in these pieces. This should have meant that they would be too vague and unfocused to be of interest to anyone. I understand now, however, that the non-specificity may be the very reason that they have endured since their publication in 2003 by Seagull Books in Kolkata. Because they are open-ended, the ideas within them can be applied, with minor adjustments, to different cultures, histories and situations.

This was demonstrated to me very recently when the set was taken up for performance in Brazil, translated into Portuguese, in November 2019. Manoela Wolff, theatre academic, writer and translator living in Porto Alegre, contacted me to seek performance permission.

She had found the monologues in her university library in *Mānoa*, the magazine of the University of Hawai'i. They had appeared in the magazine's 2010 winter issue via the guest editor of that issue - Alok Bhalla, Delhi-based poet-author, translator and retired professor of English literature, who I am lucky enough to call my friend. He had read the Seagull edition and suggested the monologues to Frank Stewart, the editor of *Mānoa*.

The result is that even as I write this introduction, these five brief performance pieces originally written in India almost twenty years ago in English are being presented in a small theatre in Porto Alegre, Brazil, in Portuguese. The performers are self-motivated and self-financed, performing only on the weekends. I find all of this deeply humbling. It's a vindication of the force of art to rise above the barriers of language, culture and distance. It also gives hope to anyone who writes in solitude, for a small publisher with no budget for publicity, wondering why it's worth bothering with these small pieces.

HIDDEN FIRES

The stage is dark. A red spotlight snaps on. A man is standing under it. He appears dishevelled with bloody bandages across his forehead and around his chest and feet. He looks over his shoulder a couple of times before he starts to speak. He is calm, but taut.

MAN: Yes ... yes! I can talk about it. Why not? I'm not ashamed. I am not afraid. Let me tell you how it was, in that first week. I was there at the beginning.

Yes – ten! That was my score. I refuse to be ashamed of it. I can explain it all – you see, they weren't really ... people. Yes, ten or ten and a half – depending on how you count the one who was pregnant. In such a situation, do we count one ... or one and a half? Or two? Anyway! The point is, ten ... *cases* were involved.

It started without warning. I was standing in my shop. One moment I was thinking about my nephew's engagement and the next moment ... there was a sound. A customer in the shop, a woman – she heard the sound before me. She said, *What's that?* Then I heard it too.

We both stepped out. We saw someone running. Behind him were seven others, maybe eight. They were carrying sticks. The one in front was running towards me. His mouth was open, no sound coming out. I knew what I had to do.

I stood in his path. He swerved to avoid me, but I held him. In that instant the boys caught up. They leapt at the man, jumped straight at him! And stamped him out.

I heard the crunch of his bones as they broke him. Scorching red juice spurted from his nose. In his final moment, he looked straight at me. The heat of his life was like a blaze in my face! And then ... he was out.

Others like this one had begun running in the streets. Some of them were female. If you want to – yes, you could call them people. I don't, of course. There's no point. That's what you don't understand. They *looked* like men, they *looked* like women. But in reality ... well ...

You have to understand. Some people are not ... people. They share the street with you and me ... but inside, deep inside ... they're not *people* ...

How else can I say it? There are some things you just know. And once you know them, you can't stop knowing them. It's like red-hot coal – it takes only one lesson to know everything you need to, about getting burnt.

You call them people? I call them red, hot coals. From an ancient fire. Not people at all. So long as they remain cool and unmoved, they're all right. But the moment they begin to smoke, the moment they show that ancient heat – then! Ah then. That's when we – we who can get burnt from that distant fire – that's when we must take action.

Who fanned those coals back to life – was it Them? Was it Us? Who set the streets aflame with them? Was it Them or was it Us? Frankly, I don't care. When a fire is raging out of control there is only one rule for dealing with it: put it out.

Here, there, everywhere ... fires were running this way and that, threatening our city, destroying our country. Some were actually aflame; others were just barely smoking. But all were burning from within, lit by their own ... otherness.

When your life's in danger, you'll do anything to defend it, won't you? When your country's in danger, you'll do anything to protect it, won't you? That's what we did.

Defended ourselves. Saved our country. We saw fires and we stamped them out.

I see it in your face – you think I did something wrong. I tell you, it was not wrong. It was right. It was the only thing to do. You would do it yourself, believe me, if you saw a fire coming your way. If you thought there was no other way to save yourself from getting burnt.

At the end of that first day, we heard the news. Two hundred dead. At the end of the next day, we heard the news. Three hundred dead. At the end of the month, we heard the news. Two thousand dead. At the end of six months, ten thousand dead.

The fire of otherness. A deadly scourge. But there's a simple rule to follow: when you see a fire, stamp it out. That first day, I counted ten. But after that day, I stopped counting. I don't know how many I killed. It became routine. Nothing very special. Like pest control. Like firefighting.

You mustn't allow yourself to be confused. Some people – you, for instance – you want to know: but HOW could I, anyone, actually kill people? So many people? I keep telling you – I didn't kill anyone. Nobody killed anybody. We saw fires and we put them out.

It's a useful approach, this one. Before, when I was still just an ordinary shopkeeper, looking after the store, minding my business, I didn't realize how simple life could be. All these years I used to think there were many laws, rules, regulations. I did as I was told. I obeyed all the rules. But now I understand: there is only one rule. When you see a fire, stamp it out.

Don't wait for help or call for the police. When you see a fire, stamp it out.

And there are a lot of fires around, believe me. Not so easy to see all of them. Some of them are hidden. Even from the people in whom they burn. It takes special eyes to see them. My eyes, for instance ... but I am starting to doubt them. At one time, everyone I saw, I knew exactly who they were. Where they came from. No longer. Now everyone wears the same clothes, the same marks on their foreheads, the same spectacles and ties ... sometimes I have trouble guessing: is that one of Them or one of Us?

I used to think, *If I don't see, immediately, from your expression or the clothes you wear or the style of jewellery around your neck or the colour of your bangles or the cut of your blouse that you are one of Us, the chances are I will assume that you're one of Them.* That's how I used to think.

It's like that amongst the animals. There are lions, there are deer. Does anyone say, *Oh, the lions are the same as the deer and the deer are the same as the lions?* No, of course not! Of course we say they are each of them different from the other!

Similarly with us. Some of us are deer, and some of us are lions. That's all there is to it. Very simple. It's normal for the lions to eat the deer. It's normal for the deer to run from the lions. After all, no one wants to be eaten. Even when it's just their ... how shall I call it? Their destiny. As deer. As prey.

It's the law of the jungle. And when the law of the jungle is broken, there is Chaos. That's what. And no one wants Chaos. Not even the deer. Ask me! I should know! I don't want Chaos. That's why I'm talking to you. Because I want to help you – to avoid Chaos, that is.

I'm sure you don't want Chaos, either. You just want to get on with your life. That's true, isn't it? It's true for me too. I'm sure you can see that. Of course you do. I am sure you'll understand, then, why I've come to you now. Why I'm standing here today. I just need a little of your time and ...

Please, no, don't turn away. Just listen to me. Please.

Till yesterday ... it was all so clear. Like I've described to you. Everything was simple. It was the law of the jungle, and I was a lion. Till yesterday. That's when they came to my house and – no, wait, please! Don't turn away!

They didn't even ask questions. They just began to beat me up. Then they threw me out of my house and set fire to my wife. She was not yet forty. They took away my sisters and their daughters. They strangled my son in front of me and pissed inside his dead mouth.

I screamed! I cried! I said, *I am one of you!* All they said was, *Hidden fires. You have hidden fires. And we've got to put them out.*

I said, *No! No! You're wrong! I have no hidden fires! I have nothing you don't have!* But they were deaf. They were blind. *Hidden fires*, they said, *we've got to put them out.*

Show me! I begged them. *Show me one sign that I am different from you!* But all they said was, *We need no reasons, don't you see? That's the law of the jungle. You believe in too, don't you? Just like we do. You say you're a lion, but your great-grandmother, three generations ago, SHE was a deer – someone told us – and that makes you a deer! And that's your hidden fire. So we've got to put you out.* Then they told me they would be kind to me. They would spare my life. Then they told me to go far away and never come back. They told me to forget about my shop, my house, my property. And that was all they said.

Don't you think it's unfair? Don't you – no! Please! Why are you turning away? Why don't you understand! There's been a mistake – isn't it obvious? Why don't you listen! They had NO REASON for beating me up! I have NO HIDDEN FIRES! If they could beat me up, they could beat you up – no, no, no! You must listen, you must! Please! It's for your own sake – believe me! If it could happen to me, it could happen to you –

Lights start to fade.

Please! Listen to me! Please! For your own sake, never mind about me – don't turn away – don't laugh and shake your head – please – listen to me – please ...

Lights and audio dim while he talks, till all that remains is a small red flickering pinpoint of light on the front of the man's chest.

I take back what I said earlier – I see that I was wrong, I was blind – I was intolerant – but it was all because I didn't understand! That's why I'm pleading with you – listen to me – it's for your own good – no! Don't turn away – don't... please ...

The small flickering light goes out too.

FAMOUS LAST WORDS

A long, horizontal display board on which twelve blank cards are displayed. The display is such that each card can be easily flipped over to expose a concealed card underneath. Each concealed card bears one letter. Each letter, when exposed, is big enough to be read from the back of the hall. At the rear of the stage is a large screen. It's black at the time the show begins. A YOUNG MAN appears.

YOUNG MAN: Ah, thank you for joining me in a game of ... FAMOUS LAST WORDS! Most of us have, at some time or another in our lives, played board games involving words and vocabulary. But tonight's game, ladies and gentlemen, isn't for the "bored" – hahaha! – no, it's for serious game-players. Deadly serious. For tonight's game I am going to ask members of the audience to call out letters. Each correct guess will register on this board. Each mistake will result in random termination of members of the audience.

Now, some of you might think that this is a cruel sort of game. You will be telling yourselves that you don't want to play. And therefore you'll remain silent. Bad news! That's not an option! Because for every minute of silence, someone belonging to the weaker sections of our society will be burnt to death. Naturally, I wouldn't want to offend the sensibilities of this audience! So I will spare you the sight of these minority deaths – and as for sound, you'll hear a small scream to punctuate each execution. As the seconds tick by, you'll see that screen at the back begin to fill up with small fires. Once the entire screen is covered in flame, your time as an audience is up: you'll ALL go up in flames.

Well, not me, of course! This is MY show. So I get to survive. And yes – I can hear some of you asking the question:

is there any way out of this disaster? Yes, there is – hey! It's a game, right? The only way out of it is to guess the right word!

So folks – are we ready? At the sound of the tone – (*pauses, as if listening to a response from the audience*) What's that? Yes, sir? What's that you said? You want to leave now, before we begin? Sorry! Not an option! Didn't they tell you, before you signed up for this show? Leaving was not an option? Because – hey! It wouldn't be much like real life, would it? I mean in real life we don't even get to decide whether or not we'll be born, never mind whether or not we'll agree to slaughter our fellow citizens when we come of age.

So this game's a little bit like real life in that sense. You don't get to make the choices when it comes to fundamental freedoms. Such as who gets to live and who gets to die. That's fixed, right? Either you're born into a society which believes in the sanctity of human life or you're not. If not, then you don't have the freedom to be squeamish! You just have to go along with whatever deck of cards is handed to you at the moment of your birth.

If you're one of the lucky ones, you're sitting in this audience and you have the right to remain alive and the right to stand by as your fellow citizens get slaughtered. If you're not so lucky, even though you're one of the lucky ones sitting in this audience tonight, you'll take the bullet for tonight's missed catches. If you're just naturally unlucky, you'll have been born into one of the countless weaker sections of our society, and might be picked off at any time and for any reason.

So! We're going to begin! The word we're looking for today is ten letters long. There's the starting tone –

Sound of the starter tone – a loud ticking commences.

– and we're off! Time's ticking away, friends – don't forget! For each minute of inaction, one person from the weaker sections is bumped off the register of life – it could be any young woman at any time, of any age, a divorcee or a widow or a mistress! It could be a Dalit, or someone in a mixed-caste, mixed-race, mixed-community marriage! It could be an old person, or an orphan or a leper! It could be an AIDS patient, a hijra or a prostitute! It could be a disabled person, a war veteran or a diabetic! It could be anyone who has a secret, anyone who is insecure, anyone who doesn't have friends or family in government service – anyone at all! So don't waste time! Don't be shy! Don't be silent! Don't be – oops!

Sound of the bell.

There's the bell –

This is followed by a pathetic shriek. In the screen at the back of the stage, one flame flickers into view.

– and there's the first victim's voice! All right folks, now you know we're not kidding! This is for real – the stakes are real, the deaths are real, the pain is real – who's gonna take a shot at that word, now, huh? Anyone? Someone? No one? So? That's how it's going to be then, people? You're going to sit back and be silent? Fine. Play it that way if you want. Because – like I told you from the start – you don't have choices. Either you let someone else burn – or you take a chance with your own skin – or you get the answers right – and if you don't make any moves at all, then, once the screen at the back fills up, you get cooked anyway! Coz that's the nature of the game. Only four choices. They die, you die, we all die or nobody dies – okay? That's what I told you at the outset – that's the way it's fixed – though of course I don't die coz I'm the one who sets the game up and I've got to remain around, right? To see that there's always an audience for the next game. And of course there's always a – oops!

Sound of the bell –

There's the bell!

– shriek, new flame in the back screen.

Another poor soul down the hatch of eternity! Never to be seen again! Never to be heard again! And you're the ones doing it, folks! It's all up to you – stay silent and they'll keep popping! Stay silent and – don't tell me I didn't warn you, okay? Coz I can tell you right now, there's no way of predicting when that screen at the back is going to fill up with flames. I know that some of you sitting in the audience are telling yourselves: *Someone else will speak up. Someone else will lose nerve and call out a letter. It doesn't have to be me, and there's a lot of space left on that screen at the back – no way it'll fill up before someone else guesses the word!* Well, let me tell you, people, you have no way of knowing how soon that screen in the back will fill up because – you know what? Fire is an unpredictable thing. Once you start a few flames off, there's no saying where the sparks will fly. No saying when suddenly, before you're prepared for it with your water cannons and your heat-proof suits, suddenly, it's YOUR roof that's on fire, YOUR daughter that's sizzling out there on the streets, YOUR parents and children and – ah! Do I see a hand? Is someone standing up back there? Is someone going to make a guess?

Silence.

Okay – okay – that's a hand I see – the gentleman in the back – what's that? Will you repeat yourself, sir? Okay! There's a guess coming in, folks! The guess is ... the letter "E"! The letter "E". And ... ohhhh dear! That letter is NOT one of those that's on my list, folks! So alas ... for making one silly mistake ... guess what? One of you is going to die. Yes, folks – that's the rule of the game – sometimes, for no reason at all, other than making the wrong guess – someone in the audience gets to die. But don't worry. Unlike the unfortunate members of our target group – hahaha! Little pun there, folks! – the audience dies by random selection.

A quick, neat bullet – don't bother ducking, anyone. It won't make the least bit of difference, if no one gets hit the first time, there'll always be a second time and a third and a fourth – until someone gets eliminated! And there's the warning buzzer –

BUZZZZZZZ!

– and there's the shot!

BOOM!

And that's one member of the audience eliminated! Hah! Isn't this exciting? It's just real life! Well, onward, onward – keep those guesses coming, folks – keep those guesses coming – don't be slow, don't be callous – it's all up to you in the end, it's a game show after all – a deadly one, a heady one – come on, come on, come on – where are those guesses, where are those hands – time's running out, folks, the clock keeps ticking – and –

Sound of the bell –

There's the bell!

– shriek, new flame in the back screen.

Oh! What a shame! Another little life dispatched forever! Gone to the celestial-dead letter box! Gone to Valhalla! No reruns! No refunds! Over and out! And the ball's back in your court, people – time to speak out, time to share – just one letter, just one try – come on folks – don't make me cry – come on, come on – where's that community spirit – where's that bleeding heart – come on, come on – time's ticking by. Ah! There you go! That's a hand! Up with that hand! Yes, Madam – what's that you said? Did I hear you right? Yes! The letter "O"! Ladies and gentlemen, the letter "O" is ... (going to the display boards) RIGHT! Here we go – here we go – not just one instance, but two! Hear that, people? This word includes two instances of the letter "O" – second from the beginning and second from the end – and what does that tell you, people, what does that tell you about the likely construction of this word, huh?

Are you wracking your brains, folks? Are you straining every nerve, now that you know your actions can result in saving lives? Yes – is that a hand I see? Over on the right – yes, Madam, speak up – what's that? Yes! "N" it is! Yes! Yes – and here's the "N" right here – right at the end of this word! Very good! Moving along, moving along! An "O" and an "N" people – what does that tell you – what does that say to you – yes – there's a hand – very good, I'm glad to see it happening, folks – I knew I could trust you – What's that you said? YES! "S" is the next one – Very good! I think you're getting the hang of it – yes, that's two "S"s in our word – and do I hear it from anyone else? Anyone willing to hazard a guess? Save some lives? That's all you need to do, folks – not very much – just stand up and make your voice heard – stand up and show that you care – stand up and try out a letter – Yes! There we go! The lady in the front! Yes – what's that you said? What? "T"? Ohhhhh. No. Ohhh. What a shame. What a shame. It isn't enough just to guess, is it? Ah no. We've got to get our guesses right, after all. Sorry about that – but you were warned – this game is for keeps, folks, and that means – yes – there's the buzzer –

BUZZZZZZ!

– another shot!

BOOM!

Another unnecessary death! Another wasted life. Oh dear, oh dear – well, onward, onward – let's keep it going, let's keep guessing folks – I like your spirit! Yes – there's another hand! And – yes! That's the correct letter! Give him a big hand, people – let him know you appreciate his spirit – the letter "P" – it's right here – right in the middle of this lovely word – yes, here we go – time's ticking away, folks, no time to spare - can't allow your mind to wander - hope you're thinking of your next word and - yes! That's another one! Yes! The letter "A"! Right here! Right next to the "P"! Very good! Excellent! And look at that, folks! Look at that word! It's almost in front of you! It's almost complete! Just two more letters and you're home and dry! Just keep trying! Just keep playing - and there's a new hand - yes, I see you - yes, I hear you - yes, there's a "C" - and here it is, right in the beginning, right at the start and there's your word, everybody - can you see it? Let me complete it for you - yes, let me give you that bonus, let me help you - here it is!

DING! DING! DING! DING! DING!

C-O-M-P-A-S-S-I-O-N - COMPASSION, everybody, yes that's the word, a good word for these bad times - Yes! And now ...

DING!

He returns to the display board and begins to flip the revealed letters up so that each display is blank once more.

... back to the display board for our NEXT word! Yes, ladies and gentlemen! The game isn't over - it's not that kind of game! Frankly, folks, did you believe that one word was going to do the trick? Can it ever be just one word, just one cure-all magic bullet? Of course not! Can there ever be just one solution? Of course not! Can we ever hope to sit back and be complacent? Of course not! So ... here we are again, people, a new word, a new set of choices ... And we'll reset that screen at the back - get ready for the bell, and all the same rules -

Sounds and lights fade out.

Thanks for playing with us tonight, folks, and stay right where you are for the next edition of FAMOUS LAST WORDS, which is about to begin ... RIGHT NOW! Okay ... an eight letter word - there's the starting tone -

Lights fade out. Curtain.

KNOW THE TRUTH!

The stage is dark. A spotlight snaps on. A YOUNG WOMAN is sitting in the posture of a newscaster. Behind her is a screen showing visuals. Except where indicated, the screen displays scenic sights or abstract patterns.

YOUNG WOMAN:

Good evening and thank you for joining us on *Know the Truth!* My name is Pranam Shanti and I will be answering your questions tonight. The topic for tonight's program is the problems affecting a few regions of our country. No one has been seriously injured! Nevertheless, our film crew will be reporting live from those areas which have been affected. We call upon ordinary citizens to share their grievances with the nation! And, as you know – operators are standing by to receive calls on this easy-to-remember number: 100-100-100.

Needless to say, our advice to all those of you who are concerned for your loved ones is: please do not worry! The government is doing its utmost to contain the violence. From all reports, it is succeeding very well. Ah, here is our first caller –

(*speaking to a caller*) Yes, Madam – yes, I can hear you clearly, please go ahead – (*listens*) Ahh ... yes ... yes ... okay.

(*to the viewers*) All right, we have a caller from ... uh ... the outskirts of a Particular City. Her name is ... well ... as you know, here at the Happy News Network we use Normal Names to protect our callers' identity – okay, so, Mrs ... uh ... Jyoti ... if I have understood your question correctly, what you want to know is, *What regions are still facing conflicts? And why can't we name the regions?*

(*smiles charmingly*) Well! That's certainly a leading question, isn't it, folks? And I'm sure some of you already have the answer ... the reason we cannot identify any of the areas where the army has been called out is, of course, that the situation is still a little uncertain. We cannot risk further instability by drawing attention to those states and towns in which a few unrelated incidents of violence have occurred. In the past, when we followed the policy of revealing everything there is to know about a situation, it only resulted in prolonging the chaos. Nevertheless, in our bid to bring the Truth home to you, in a few seconds we will show you live footage from one of the affected areas. Here it is now – live coverage – a simple rural scene ... no sign of any disturbance ...

Visual shows a crowded marketplace in Rajasthan. It is the Pushkar Fair and colourful Rajasthani villagers are shown haggling over camels. It is a standard tourist brochure shot and there is no sign of any disturbance anywhere.

(*continuing to the viewers*) As you can see, everyone looks perfectly healthy and there is no longer any sign of the bloodshed – except for this one person, a child of ten – who has a minor cut on his elbow –

Visual shows a shot taken in a studio of a child actor dressed in Rajasthani peasant clothes. He is holding up his elbow, which has been covered in a huge white bed sheet with red ink splashed on it to suggest blood.

(*to the unseen, unheard caller*) I hope that satisfies you, Mrs ... uhhh ... Jyoti! Thank you for your call – and – here's our next caller now – yes, sir, yes – please go ahead, I can hear you perfectly well – (*listens*) – yes – okay – I think I understand what you want to know – okay, okay, please be patient, sir – it takes a little time to ... uh ... to understand the nature of your concern. Yes – please, okay – okay – I'll get back to you, sir –

(*to the viewers, slightly ruffled*) Well ... that was Mr ... Mr ... Haz – uh – Anand ... and his question is, *What ... what is the government doing about the ... the disturbance on the street where I live?* He ... he wanted me to say that he lives in a ...

Particular City ... on the west coast of India and that he's had a ... uhhh ... small problem with the ... uhhh ... water supply for the past few ... uh ... hours.

(*to the viewers, but as if also speaking to "Mr Anand"*) Now, you see, Mr Anand, I understand your problem, but the fact is, according to our sources, there is practically no disruption of vital supplies happening in your area of the country! So I am at a loss to explain what the matter is in your house. Is it possible that there is some absolutely ... you know ... LOCAL problem? A car accident or something like that? Because that too can, you know, cause situations in which citizens can be inconvenienced.

So ... I hope that answers your query, Mr Anand – and I'm sure your wife and children will be returned to you very shortly – after all, the government has given an absolute assurance that no violence will be tolerated after 8 p.m. on weekdays. Thank you for calling! And here's our next caller now –

SFX: A loud crackling and the sound of static. Abrupt cessation of the call.

(*to the viewers, looking startled*) Oh! Well, that was sudden – and now we seem to have lost our connection briefly – no problem! We'll just wait till our engineers restore it! And while we wait, let me play for you a message direct from one of our leaders:

Visual shows a politician speaking into a microphone.

VOICE-OVER, POLITICIAN:

... inform the people of our beloved country that there is ABSOLUTELY NOTHING TO FEAR! The government has been completely successful in its campaign to end terror within the nation's borders. There have been no live burnings or gang rapes in any of the disputed territories in the past six hours. Telecasts and radio broadcasts from foreign news agencies MUST BE IGNORED. As we know, foreigners have for centuries followed a policy of maligning the people and culture of our nation. It is of utmost importance that we resist their vile propaganda and remain faithful to the Real Truth – which is that there is nothing bad happening within our borders at all. We are committed to the path of peaceful and non-violent suppression of all anti-national behaviour. We ask only for a little patience – after all, such disturbances are a natural part of Nation Building. We are determined to bring the situation under control in the shortest possible time. So long as all our citizens avoid overreacting when they are faced with mobs or rapist gangs, so long as they maintain a patriotic silence when approached by foreign news agencies, we are certain that complete normalcy will be restored in less than half a year. JAI HIND!

YOUNG WOMAN:

And that message was from one of our leaders, speaking from an undisclosed location somewhere in the world. Now! Back to our regular broadcast of calls from around the nation! Yes – and there's a caller – that's – okay, Puja Arora – hello, Puja! Thank you for calling! I recognize your voice from last week. Why don't you share your good news again with all our listeners today?

Visual of a sweet young girl.

VOICE-OVER, CHILD:

Auntie, I want to share my experience with your audience! My name is Puja and I am fifteen years old. The Particular City in which I am living is absolutely safe, and totally quiet! Nothing goes wrong and we are all living in communal harmony! We have no problems with power or water! Only happy people are walking in the streets and in the morning we read only good news in the newspaper! Every day, when I go to school, I am very happy to see my teacher and my friends! We have a lot to eat and we study very hard! All my friends in my city are happy and healthy and we are very proud of our country. My teacher says there is no country better than our country and when I grow up, I'll be a teacher too! Or a doctor or a nurse or an engineer, so that I can serve my country better. I will be glad to give my life for my country if I get the chance. Thank you, auntie, thank you for giving me the opportunity to share my real, true feelings with all my fellow citizens in my world's best country!

YOUNG WOMAN:

Awww! Wasn't that sweet? Wasn't that heart-warming? Thank you, Puja, I am certain all our viewers were deeply touched by your emotional message! We all need to hear the good news too – that's what we feel, here at *KNOW THE TRUTH!* – after all, let's not forget: for every riot or rape, there's still some sunshine somewhere! Yes, my friends! Let's concentrate on the cheers, not the tears! That's our motto! Forget the sadness of the past and focus on the gladness of the future!

(*speaking to a caller*) And here's our next caller. Yes, Madam, please go ahead. Yes, I can hear you – of course, please keep talking –

(*looking sympathetic*) Okay ... and that's Ms Khush Boo calling from a – uhhh – Particular City! Yes, Ms Khush Boo – keep talking, I can hear you – what's that? Are those ... uhh ... firecrackers I hear? What? Oh ... well, how can you be sure, Ms Boo? Sometimes firecrackers DO sound like bombs! Ah well – just keep smiling and try to stay positive – I'm sure the police will come soon – or the army – whatever – the main point is, KEEP SMILING! Okay?

(*nodding her head understandingly*) I know, I know – it's very difficult in these troubled times, Ms Boo, to keep your spirits high – what's that? They're breaking down your neighbour's door? Ohh ... I'm sure you're only imagining it! It can't be happening, really it can't! The government has ASSURED us there is no violence in your Particular City!

Really, Ms Khush Boo, perhaps you're just imagining it? After all, young people like you DO have very active minds! – Awww ... well, don't feel too bad ... okay, Ms Khush Boo – remember what I said, think positive thoughts! And maybe the bad men will go away ... Sorry, no, I can't keep you on the line, as I need to get on with the show – bye-bye now – thanks for calling –

(*smiling at her viewers*) – and that was a young caller complaining about some recurring nightmares she has! Poor thing – she imagines that all the young women on her street have been raped and/or murdered – now isn't that just impossible, folks? That can't happen in our country, am I right? And now she thinks there's a mob at her door! Poor thing! Ohh ... delusions can be terrible, can't they? We at *Know the Truth!* are always keen to keep our delusions at bay. We just keep on smiling and telling people the truth and though it's not always easy, as we all know, in the end, the truth DOES prevail!

And that's all for today! Thank you for watching! Tune in again every hour on the hour for the next edition of ... *KNOW THE TRUTH!*

Lights fade out. Curtain.

POINTS

A young woman appears onstage. She is carrying an unlit candle in her right hand.

YOUNG WOMAN:

Can everyone see this candle? (*she holds it up high*)

Okay ... (*she kneels down on the ground and lights the candle*) In case some of you can't see me, I'll tell you what I'm doing – I'm lighting this candle ... (*she does so*) Okay! It's lit.

(*gets to her feet, holding the lit candle in her hand*) Everyone, please, I want you to look at this candle, look at the flame.

The flame represents the spirit of my country.

Now some of you may think you know what I mean when I say "my country" – and maybe you're right. But just in case you're not, I'll tell you what I mean when I say "my country".

To begin with, it's not a political region. It has no boundaries, no visa offices, no armies to defend it. My country is the earth we stand upon when we step outside our homes. My country is the air we breathe when we stand under the sun.

My second point is that my country is ALSO a political region. It has boundaries, it sells visas, it has an army. But these things do not define it. These things are part of what it has.

My third point is about ownership. I belong to my country. But it does not belong to me. Or to anyone else. Nobody can take it away or bring it back – it has volume, it has area, it has value – but all of these are uncertain quantities.

They change from moment to moment. They are not what define my country. One dimension alone is important: my country exists in time. It has a beginning.

My fourth point is about beginning. My country began when the earth of which it is made, began. The plants with which it peopled itself were its first citizens. We do not know by what stages its subsequent citizens arrived. We can only guess.

My fifth point is about guessing. When we guess who we were before we were ourselves, we can only make mistakes. There is no saying which part of what we are today was there in the beginning. Matter is neither created nor destroyed, it is merely rearranged. We are, all of us, rearrangements of matter.

My sixth point is about rearrangements. Plants are rearrangements of air, water, sunlight and organic molecules. Animals who eat the plants are rearrangements of the plants. Animals who eat animals are rearrangements of those who eat the plants. Human beings eat animals and plants. We are all rearrangements of something else.

My seventh point is about something else. We are something other than the physical matter of which we are made. We are also the words we speak and the thoughts in our minds, and our feelings and our ideas. We are also our moods and our desires, our personalities and our hopes. We are also the breath that animates our lives. We are also composed of matter that cannot be measured by weight or height.

What is the weight of a word? Or the dimension of a thought? How do we measure those things which exist beyond measurement? How do we capture what cannot be grasped?

So my eighth point is about that which cannot be grasped. The insubstantial essence of ourselves. Like the flame of this candle in my hand. Like the spirits of living beings. These are not elements that can be measured or quantified. No value can be placed on them in terms of money. Yet they are real and they exist. Like this flame is real, even though I cannot grasp it, tie it down or own it.

My ninth point is about reality. We all know what reality is, even if we cannot grasp it, or tie it down or own it. Reality is the sum of everything without being any one thing. Reality is the flame of a candle of which we ... are the wick.

I have no more points to make.

She extinguishes the candle. Curtain.

INVOCATION

The stage is bare except for a display of lights in the centre – a board on which 1,000 fairy lights are visible and lit. A figure appears, walks up to the front of the stage so that she is framed by the fairy lights displayed behind her. As she begins to read the names, the lights begin to go out, forty at a time, between pauses. She addresses the audience directly.

FIGURE: I am going to read out a list of one thousand names. Anyone who hears his or her name is welcome to raise his or her hand for a few moments. That way, we'll know who's with us today.

Here are the first forty:

Duggal Jaiswal Sabharwal Vimal Rawail Kapil Savitri Jethari Nathani Banwari Jhalani Watwani Sati Srichand Choria Shakalaya Suneja Palwa Rantela Durga Kuswaha Racchoya Vidya Bahuguna Arora Rajan Mohan Sarjan Cabrihan Harbans Maggu Brijesh Ashif Fanthome Gaur Nahar Attar Kuldip Amarjeet Upadhyay

I got the majority out of the New Delhi telephone directory. I opened each of the two volumes in the middle, then I used a needle to pierce all the way through one side of the directory, then the other side. Perhaps some of you are wondering how I managed to push a needle all the way through a telephone directory?

But first, another forty names:

Babar Johar Amar Brar Bansal Uppal Karnal Sabal Shakuntala Srivastava Arneja Paharia Mobina Mukundan Dutta Jana Samanta Chanana Nazrul Virmani Faridi Ghazi Jaswati Virji Bhagwani Sawhney Sabir Quanungo Madho Arun Hardev Ehtesham Ismail Jitender Mulk Rawat Ussan Kalhan Sunil Raj

Well, the answer to the mystery of the needle is that I used a small hammer. I drove the needle in 20 or 30 pages at a time until there was a tiny puncture mark through every page. Then I just noted down the names that appeared closest to the puncture marks.

Now another forty names:

Arjan Haridasan Karan Ebraham Jaskaran Madan Sanan Allen Stephen Saxena Charia Gainda Sunita Usha Bora Virgotra Murasha Valsa Chaliha Bhageria Jindal Mittal Joel Nimwal Satyarthi Elawadi Qureshi Banerjee Sachdev Rais Girdhar Vishwamitter Opinder Jat Tambe Sukhatme Azad Anwar Reginold Kulwant

I ignored names which had already been entered in my list, preferring, as far as possible, not to repeat any. It's not always easy to do that: sometimes a name will appear several times, in different places in the directory, with alternate spellings.

And here's another forty names:

Jiva Chhabra Raheja Mishra Qudsia Wadia Banarsi Vadami Upretti Bhaduri Ansari Alamelu Sadhu Anu Francis Biswas Jaswant Sawant Dushyant Suraj Om Lynnus Nitin Wad Harjinder Kashal Gopal Santhanam Venkatraman Kumar Chajjer Shanker Avdesh Ralhan Scott Subhash Johnson Jatav Virk Mustak

That takes us up to one hundred and sixty names.

So anyway ... I wrote down the names in columns of forty, allowing five columns per sheet of A4 paper. That meant five sheets of paper. Once I had my basic list, I redistributed the names so that they were no longer in strict alphabetical order. I did this by copying them out from the columns on to visiting cards – twenty-five blank visiting cards. I entered the names on to the cards, reading across the columns, line by line.

Time for another forty names!

Gambhir Mir Sarup Anoop Ajmer Sagar Sharma Suresh Asirvathan Vijaraghavan Sudan Johan Balwan Harkrishan Benjamin Vaijayanti Padmini Udhani Doji Piplani Kundra Luthra Seetha Kathuria Nalkha Budhiraja Anita Wahal Bisht Charanjit Gopinath Inyat Jose Vendil Rajpal Sehgal Jay Chet Raghubir Oberoi

Once they were on the cards, I began copying them into my computer. It wasn't possible to pull out one thousand unique names using the needle system alone. So I chose a further ninety names by just searching through the directory for those which weren't already on my list. Once the names were in my computer, I rearranged them slightly, so that they would be easier to read out loud.

And now, another forty:

Chawla Birla Sudha Walia Ira Goyanka Kushwala Thadani Wahi Patni Gandhi Bedi Rizvi Sembhi Balmiki Varandani Nizami Mighlani Lohri Seistani Jolly Sahai Jhun Surgian Udyan Paliwal Patel Harpal Katyal Nagpal Mangal Dobriyal Anil Wasif Animesh Pinto Joy Sarkar Ajit Radhe

I looked only for surnames and for the most part, I used the directory's main entries, the ones that appear in bold letters. So even though some names on my list appear to be first names, I included them because that's how they appeared in the directory. Wherever I made mistakes or found names that I had mistakenly entered twice, I substituted them with the names of my friends – being careful, of course, to include my own.

Another forty coming up:

Ganga Juneja Dudeja Nirmala Kapurthala Nagia Pincha Kaila Manchanda Bawa Aneja Gangoli Bali Haveli Suri Puthi Likhari Irani Gulani Dakshini Rohatgi Jit Menon Panwar Shahid Yad Bindlish Sujjan Padmanabhan

Chauhan Kaushal Pathak Shat Serwat Vaseem Ajay Ugrasen Xavier Sahu Thakur

It's important that you know by what method I chose the names on my list because if I didn't tell you, you'd want to know what my selection criterion was when I explain WHY I went to this effort.

But first, another forty names:

Dua Mehta Batra Lata Ahuja Sheila Bimla Chamalia Zatharia Thapa Wasuja Purshottam Niranjan Saini Vasi Roopwati Shakti Yogi Guliani Hemrajani Passi Kawal Olak Kanith Amrit Toshiwal Nag Namgain Anand Seth Sukhesh Chaudhary Kailash Baldev Ganjoo Garg Hinwar Parihar Joginder Surinder

Well, and that takes us to three hundred and twenty. Another six hundred and eighty to go. Another seventeen pauses.

Now I am going to discuss the three reasons for which I put this list together. The first reason is that I wanted to make an invocation. By invocation, I mean, just as we invoke the gods by reciting their thousand names, I am reciting one thousand names of real people, in order to invoke the gods of a democracy - that is, the people. The gods of a democracy are the people. I am invoking the power of the people, to listen - listen to this protest.

Here's another forty names:

Gauba Dora Sakhuja Mehra Lamba Thimmaiyya Tota Chaturvedi Puri Bihari Chari Oli Kalawati Hingorani Joshi Shetty Kamat Balbir Ahmed Nigam Zubir Amrit Shansuddin Hisamuddin Gulwinder Abhyankar Kehar Mutatkar Basrar Jokhar Yadav Parvesh Malik Amrik Surjeet Parmjeet Roy Shadab Sultan Vats

The protest is my second reason for putting this list together. My protest concerns the names that are missing from the public record. Do you notice how when there's a riot, we are rarely told who died? Instead, we are given numbers. We're given details of the property that was damaged. We are offered glimpses of who may have been responsible. But we are rarely shown the names of those who died.

But, meanwhile, here's another forty names:

Toteja Bejana Bala Sharda Dogra Julka Malhotra Barua Rungta Gauri Negi Chatterjee Amrohi Kalsi Murli Kansal Dyal Kewal Chaswal Thukral Ahlawat Salman Shiv Sushil Ved Puran Mehar Lalit Permananad Bhowmick Oliver Gurbaksh Hiroo Yag Parveen Ambesh Shah Summan Gautam Human

A name is a powerful thing. It's the first thing we get when we are born. It's one of the few things that survives us when we die, continuing to exert an influence through wills and land records and tombstones. It's a handle by which we can be controlled as well as a tool with which some of us control others. To invoke the name of a powerful bureaucrat, for example, is to invoke the powers of that bureaucrat's office. A name is a passport across the borders of reality, which shows who we are, where we came from and to whom we belong.

Now here are more names:

Bhojwani Nihalani Ghai Dimpi Phoolwati Kamini Bakshi Ali Kapadia Saluja Sushma Charkha Veena Meena Hoda Handa Dehalla Pundlik Neelkandhan Malkan Bishan Shivrajan Aggarwal Lal Munjal Sheelawant Dixit Imamuddin Khalid Noor Gurcharanjeet Sualaheen Tilak Parshant Yesh Harish Keshav George Kad Chansarkar

We speak of people being "twice born": the first is their physical birth into this world and the second is their birth into their faith. The victims of riots, by contrast, might be called "twice dead": they die a physical death in the streets and a second death in the public record. We know of them only as statistics. Unlike soldiers who die in a war, unlike passengers who die in aircraft accidents, these victims of violence pass out of our consciousness as if their deaths were of no account.

Here's another forty names:

Dhuna Daya Chandra Bhayana Maknotra Gullah Adlakha Venugopal Pritpal Nonihal Pratipal Kariwal Iqbal Bakhtawar Mazhar Kakar Swaran Khan Sampuran Kanan Binani Khattari Shri Damani Mulseri Naveen Lakshmi Ghasi Shenoy Dil Aklesh Chatrath Gurmeet Subendu Tokas Yusaf Parkash Karjit Haradhat Ghose

I'm sure, if you or I were killed in mob violence, we would hope, in our final moments, that we would at the very least be remembered by our fellow citizens. A victim of mob violence dies defending his or her right to exist. He or she becomes a martyr to the cause of human dignity. But unlike other martyrs, riot victims are not memorialized: at the very most, the few who have surviving family members are referred to in passing, in press interviews, after the event.

Time for more names:

Gian Pritam Subhan Dhiwan Jayan Kalia Verma Khera Bishwa Kanojia Shriniwas Prithviraj Dhir Kartar Majumdar Dawar Bajaj Ishwardas Hemraj Khandelwal Gurpal Abrol Chandhok Syed Sandhu Nathu Matoo Toor Shish Vakil Zamruddin Parikh Bijlani Gingee Lakhi Barti Airy Nomani Hari Mukherjee

State authorities and governments are not likely to publicize the names of those who died in violent riots, or to make an effort to inscribe their names in granite, or to create memorial sites to them. Why? Because a riot is a disgrace to the nation in which it occurs. By refusing to acknowledge those who die, we are, in effect, trying to keep the record clean.

Yet more names:

Kalra Khanna Dasgupta Bismillah Kanta Ladda Trikha Shukla Kataria Dhingra Baikunth Abdul Mathur Sangi Pulyani Vidyawati Maini Hothi Bhutani Prem Naseem Shokeen Bhanot Agyakar Tahir Issar Gurvinder Gullu Ranjodh Haryal Pardeep Rakesh Mukesh Harisharan Girijan Khimanand Mirjan Dhiman Gobind Chander

So that brings me to my third reason for putting together this list of one thousand names. They are meant to stand proxy for the names of the dead. Since we will not be shown the names of those who really died, and since we will not be given an opportunity to mourn the real violence of those deaths, I have put together a list of names, chosen randomly, as symbolic of the names we will not be shown.

Here's another forty names.

Bissa Rabiya Talla Gogia Kharbanda Preeta Narula Katnala Chopra Goel Bahl Kamal Dhanwal Kanwar Dhawan Darshan Bhushan Jagan Bhajan Modak Mrinal Harnam Ram Shyam Chand Sanjay Somani Farshori Rantri Indrawati Trilokhi Vij Khursheed Hakim Rajveer Paramjit Tikkoo Mathur Aganpul Jacob

Some of you may feel that it's unfair to use names from a telephone directory, of people who are most likely alive, to take the place of those who are dead. But look at it this way: violent riots are unfair too. Those deaths occur randomly too – to people whose names and identities suddenly turn malignant upon them, because of circumstances beyond their control.

Here's another forty names:

Gopalan Chaman Sugan Mannon Morrison Bhagwan Gonga Bagha Sidana Lanka Raina Dhameja Adkana Papna Hadija Dareja Bhupendra Rajpal Khattar Talwar Prasad Kamlesh Dhaundiyal Kaul Kiran Ramadurai Vijay Maheshwari Sansi Jaggi Massey Narsingh Mobin Islamuddin Rohtash Thomas Dagar Balwinder Birgu Triyug

And that brings us to six hundred and forty. Another three hundred and sixty to go.

Some of you may feel, with particular reference to the riots in Gujarat, that these names I've been reading out are not appropriate. Because of differences in religion and ethnicity, only a few of them are likely to be similar to the names of those who died in Gujarat. Before you jump to hasty conclusions, however, here's another forty names:

Monga Bhola Tibrewala Dhalia Tamta Vijendra Anchalia Hina Marwah Letha Gostwal Kanhayalal Dharamvir Jagveer Chakrabarti Sidhwani Bagai Tuseer Jagdeep Ramavatar Ketarpal Lambardar Manzar Santosh Pramod Navinder Rajeshwari Sukhcharan Bhagat Gosain Kaushik Abraham Kishore Roshan Dabas Balasubramaniam Rajnish Pannu Mahesh Dang

It's true that when I started compiling these names my aim was to protest against the riots in Gujarat. Let me be clear: my aim was to protest the deaths in the train compartment in Godhra equally with the deaths on the streets of Ahmedabad and elsewhere. But as my list began to fill out, I asked myself, *Why should this be a protest only against the recent riots?* Why discriminate between riots?

Here's another forty names:

Kanwal Sappal Dhanda Chadha Simha Bariwala Durga Lohia Kotia Sukija Baby Ramesh Tandon Vinay Prabhu Naresh Maqsood Rajeet Deveshwar Jainti Jagdish Khullar Anchan Langan Balkishan Mayal Sachan Rajgopalan Irkey

Christy Tyagi Maharishi Govil Grover Pandit Daljit Mohsin Kazim Ibrahim Bhim

So, I began to think of all the violence we have heard about and been witness to: the bomb blasts in Bombay and the riots which followed them. The anti-Sikh riots and the violence in Kashmir; the riots in Assam and the killings by and of Naxalites, the decimation of tribals, and the horror of Partition.

Here's another forty names:

Gulabrani Popli Bakshi Ubhi Bhattacharjee Jaitley Bablani Raniji Chiranjiv Bumrah Khurana Sadana Behura Dutta Gulia Taneja Saraf Mahajan Dhall Singhal Andhiwal Narang Manoj Vinod Magazine Khainiddin Sumer Tomar Deshraj Krishnan Raman Mehan Langoo Kapoor Rajesh Pande Mohinder Jagirdar Inderjeet Dalel

Then I began to think of all the other deaths that have occurred, elsewhere in the world, of people whose names have passed out of the sunlight of life and into the vaults of unmemory.

The victims in Bangladesh, in Kosovo, in Sri Lanka, in Afghanistan, in Iran, Iraq, Indonesia and the Philippines, in China, in Argentina, in Rwanda, Nigeria, the Congo and South Africa, in Vietnam, in Cambodia, in the plains of North America, in the jungles of South America, in the deserts of Australia ... how endless is this list! How heavy with unremembered blood!

Here's another forty names:

Lekwani Mangi Bajpai Gulati Karakothi Viranwali Kulkarni Ramdevi Sarat Singh Tanveer Safiq Narain Manohar Chhibbar Rajender Podar Baba Rana Kindra Dahuja Palta Malgotra Surekha Bawalia Ekka Anotra Khangwal Umarwal Jaman Jagnandan Trehan Gurbachan Dewan Mohammed Mahabeer Isaac Bhatt Dev Budh

That brings us to eight hundred. Two hundred to go.

If there is one lesson that the Jews of Hitler's Germany have taught us, it is the value of remembrance. Six million died in Europe, but their names have not been forgotten. Those deaths continue to resonate amongst our lives, as a remembrance to what must not be allowed to happen again. Those names have become a form of capital against which a currency of justice has been minted.

Here's another forty names:

Gulshan Kashyap Devrajan Brij Awasthi Ranbir Sarat Desai Tapar Virender Mahar Randhawa Nangia Manocha Phutela Daya Batheja Bahuguna Khemka Midha Saha Ratha Sushant Farooqi Sohani Jaisinghani Madhyani Jang Kumbhat Zakir Trilok Chattar Bharathan Ashok Satbir Jad Kishan Dabas Bhatnagar Gurdial

My list of one thousand names is as nothing compared to the list that would be generated if all the names that belonged on it were to be uttered. It is tedious enough to listen to one thousand names being recited. Imagine if we could hear the complete list. My list is a fragile, audio-memorial to all those whose own names became their death sentence, all those whose names we will not hear. It is meant to be a reminder, and a warning.

Here's another forty names:

Solomon Gurmukh Rangroo Gupta Batliwala Nanda Bhatia Tulika Kathpalia Asha Fuloria Mahna Khosla Sinha Satinder Devinder Vishamber Avtar Bouns Sarin Tarsem Ravindran Takhat Dave Bashal Jaspal Manmohan Kunti Zakiuddin Nakar Kohli Chuni Sahi Chandwani Peshwari Bahi Bharadwaj Rathor Jalan Jagdish

Because, in case we don't realize it, let me also point out that my list, that I compiled out of the New Delhi telephone directory, could in a moment of blindness and misjudgement – just one nuclear bomb, for instance – turn into a list of victims.

Here are another forty names:

Hafiz Gurbir Katyayan Devi Kirplani Sirohi Atri Namboodari Rehmani Taragi Zalani Jasbi Koshy Sondi Ranjit Vivekanand Pawar Bhanwar Bhasker Dar Manju Mam Gajanand Javed Kuthiala Ojha Mittar Bodhan Sailaja Chandola Bagga Arya Sarla Baria Tayal Ujlayan Rattan Satish Sitaram Chugh

Only eighty names left to go, by the way.

At any moment, the comfort and security you know might be shattered – by an unfortunate choice of residence, a quirk of spelling – factors that have little to do with your personal choice – your life might suddenly be reduced to a charred husk, with all your futures and your pasts laid to waste.

Here's another forty names:

Hans Bisht Ganpat Kutar Wattan Pawan Unnikrishnan Chanderen Gurkirpal Deswal Kocchar Assudaney Tekchandani Tawdey Damyanti Bansi Qudri Bhandari Ravi Soni Jai Rao Saroj Skariah Saira Vohra Kaushalya D'Souza Renuka Nair Manjit Jaraman Mor Badlu Arvind Satwant Jaswinder Godrej Ray Bhasin

Against such a circumstance and as a prayer that such a moment will not be visited upon you, or me, or anyone of these thousand names – and the thousand, million, billion other names that these names are supposed to stand in symbolic representation of – I make this invocation. In the names of ourselves, in the powers invested in us as citizens of a free nation, I make this invocation. In the names of those who have already died, I make this invocation.

Here are my final forty names:

Harbhajan Gurusharan Wadhwan Bishan Kaval Dehall Ashwani Rastogi Sodhi Tewari Nahid Manglam Manmeet Rohella Tejan Paul Dal Banik Garib Jha Kuti Qadri Krishnamurthy Watts Moulik Babu Saryu Arshad Sood Ravinder Johar Jain Bhargava Bhambra Salarpuria Urmila Chandela Kukreja Chittkara Satya

Let us be done with violence. Let those who have indulged in violence be named and punished. Let those who have died in violence be named and remembered.

With this, I end my invocation.

Curtain.

Introduction

The Cook's Story, The Dhobi's Wife, Ladies' Night, The Rape Artist, Blind Date

These five shorts are not really a group; more like two pairs and a one-off. The first pair concerns domestic help, the second pair is about rape. The last one is a piece of random weirdness. Very loosely though, they are each about people and perspectives we don't often think about.

The Cook's Story and *The Dhobi's Wife* were inspired by my ongoing interest in domestic helpers. Their position, so intimately threaded into the fabric of middle-class homes whilst also remaining entirely locked out, should be worth much more attention than it normally gets. I would've liked to write a third piece, to make it a set, but never got around to it.

The Dhobi's Wife represents a thought that has tickled my imagination for many years: that the clothes' washers in a home must surely have an insight into the least public aspects of a family's life. In the age before washing machines they saw the stains and creases of the family as a whole. Plus, when we're talking of professional dhobis, who collect and deliver clothes on a weekly basis, they see all manner of intimate apparel, bed and table linen week to week. They could, if they wanted, compile a forensic portrait of the inmates of a home, based entirely on the trail of soiled and unsoiled clothes. I don't know whether Indian soap operas have made ample use of this fact in their narratives but I would expect they must have.

I read *The Cook's Story* to a small audience of senior school students in Kodaikanal once in 2008. Aside from that, both these pieces have remained unseen. The cook of the piece isn't based on anyone known to me. I grew up with male cooks, bearers and drivers. Their constant presence was a pleasant but unremarkable part of my childhood. I was quite amazed to realize, in my early twenties, that live-in domestic helpers were exceptions around the world, not the norm.

I wrote *Ladies' Night* and *The Rape Artist* for a two-day event organized by the Seagull Foundation in Kolkata in 2013. In the months following the infamous December 2012 gang rape and murder in New Delhi there were many efforts made around the country to focus on the atmosphere of violence against women. I and Megha Malhotra of Seagull read the two short scripts out to a small audience. The pieces were received with friendly but somewhat puzzled attention. It's possible that they would get a very different reception today, in our post-#MeToo world.

They must, I think, be presented in tandem. They are like the tragedy-comedy masks of theatre: one is almost ghastly and the other is almost funny. *The Rape Artist* examines rape from the diseased perspective of a twisted young man; *Ladies' Night* is a light fantasy about a form of vigilantism that has yet to be attempted on Indian streets (or anywhere else, so far as I know).

Blind Date is a piece that has three catalysts. One was *The Sextet*. At the time I wrote that set, several tangential ideas occurred to me, of further short performance pieces on themes of gender, identity and dysfunction.

I have had a long-standing interest in the science of reproduction, inheritance and genetics. I knew, for instance, that conjoined twins cannot be of mixed gender. So far as I know, there cannot be conjoined or even identical triplets. Sets of three are composed of one set of identical twins and one fraternal sibling, or else three fraternal siblings, born at the same time (I don't know if recent developments in conception technology have changed what was once bedrock fact).

The second catalyst was, frankly, ridiculous. I had read a notice in an online theatre magazine in the US inviting entries for a "Worst Play Script" competition. That sounded to me like a very odd proposition. After all, who would want to win such a competition? Would the result be good theatre nevertheless? Who would decide? But before I could dismiss the idea, the memory of the triplets returned to me. This time there was a definite structure. They would be mixed-gender-conjoined, waiting on a street corner to meet an opposite-mixed-gender-conjoined on a blind date.

I wrote a first draft of the piece, meaning the first three pages, right away, sometime in 2008. Then, for a very long time, I could not push myself beyond the opening premise. I had three individual beings trapped in one body, a brother between two sisters. And that was all. I hadn't firmed up the exact arrangement of their limbs. I couldn't decide how I would disentangle their personalities. I didn't know what the blind date would be like: successful, unsuccessful, funny, sad or ridiculous.

Most importantly, I didn't have a "why" for the piece as a whole. The desire to write something irreverent with a gendered theme was, of course, always lurking but that was no longer enough. There had to be something more.

In my view, conjoined individuals are only the physical version of what many of us experience in a metaphysical sense. That is, the vast majority of us live with our parents and siblings permanently embedded within our minds. Most of us do not think of this as unusual or undesirable. It only becomes undesirable when, and if, it turns toxic. If that happens, there's no escape. No surgery can remove a parent or sibling embedded in one's mind.

Knowing this, however, wasn't enough of a reason to complete the piece. Enter, then, the third catalyst: an invitation from Shirley Huston-Findley, professor of theatre at the College of Wooster in Ohio, to contribute to an anthology of plays by Indian women playwrights that she was compiling. She had already researched and included a collection of interviews with Indian women playwrights, of which I was one. The plays would be added with the interviews.

I showed her *The Wish* but said that I had another piece I wanted to develop specifically for her anthology. I told her its name and gave her a brief description. She said she'd like to wait for it, whereupon the remaining twenty-odd pages of *Blind Date* leapt out as if they had only been waiting for this curtain call.

Shirley's compilation, *Disparate Voices of Indian Women Playwrights*, has just been published and I received my contributor's copy in the mail yesterday, while writing this introduction. It's very odd to see *Blind Date*, this little playlet that began under the least promising auspices, suddenly visible in cold print. Parts of this introduction are taken from the note I wrote to accompany my script at the time of submission.

I have shown *Blind Date* to two very different people. One pronounced it "good fun!" right away. The other hated it so much that she advised me to smother it under a pillow immediately.

As I write this, I have no way of knowing if it could ever work onstage. I don't know if any actors would be able to overcome the difficulties of simulating a three-way conjoined existence. I don't know if the finished result would be worth the effort. Still. I am already thinking about those other cheeky and immoderate ideas that appeared alongside this one, many years ago.

THE COOK'S STORY

The COOK is a man of middle height. He is spare, neat and old. Thinning hair slicked back, dyed black; thin moustache; white-on-white uniform of bush shirt and pants. He stands behind a kitchen counter, cutting vegetables.

COOK: (*speaking as if to a child standing in front of the counter*) So. You're the new boy, huh? Very good. (*chuckles*)

And they've sent you to me. Ohh yes. Of course they've sent you to me! I can tell you all you'll need to know about working in this house.

He is cutting an onion, very slowly and carefully.

I might tell you more than you need to know ... but that's a risk you'll have to take, if you listen to me. Of course, you don't have to listen. But then again, what do you lose? A little time, that's all. And we servants, we're rich when it comes to time, aren't we? Too bad it's such a common commodity. Or we might get a better price for it ... (*chuckles*)

I came here after the old cook had died. The Old Madam – she was young then – wanted a little boy. Someone she could "train up". Someone small and fresh. Full of juice.

(*chuckles*) I was just like you when I came here – a little cricket! Hungry. Always hungry. My uncle worked next door as a driver. The day the old cook died, my uncle came straight to the village to fetch me.

My mother was so happy! One mouth less to feed. I was happy too. How many village boys get a chance to work in a big house like this one? Not many.

Been here ever since. Seen the children of the house grow up, get married, have children of their own. I got married too. Had children of my own too. (*shrugs*) I hardly see them, of course. My wife lives in the village. (*shrugs*) I hardly see her either.

(*chuckles*) The wheel of life! It'll run you over like a dog in the street, if you don't watch out!

Anyway. Where was I? The Old Madam. She was kind to me. She let me sleep in her sons' room. Two little boys, they were, when I came. Eight and ten years old. If they woke up at night, I would bring them water. I would take them to the toilet. I would watch their dreams flickering under their eyelids.

Sometimes the power went off. When that happened, I could sit inside their mosquito net, at the foot of the bed, fanning those two. Otherwise, I slept on the bare floor. I didn't mind.

I used to help them with their uniforms, polish their shoes, carry their bags to the car ... When they came back from school they would play with me. Sometimes I was the ball. Sometimes I was the bat. Either way, I was beaten. I didn't mind.

I was given their old clothes to wear. When they grew up, I grew up. I began sleeping in the servants' quarter. I had my own room, imagine! No fan, no bed, just a bare room. But I was happy. It was more than I had ever had.

My duty was from six in the morning till six the next morning, every day. If there was a party, I stayed up until it was over. I stayed here all throughout: when the Old Madam died and the younger boy brought his wife home to live here, when the Old Master died and the older boy and his wife came to live in the house. Now they all live together. For all of them, I do the cooking.

You're probably wondering – aren't you? – why am I telling you about people? What do they have to do with your cooking?

I'll tell you: everything.

Because the food that passes through a cook's hands turns into the people he works for. Ever thought of that? No? But it's true, isn't it?

Picking up an onion he has not yet peeled.

See this onion? It looks like an onion now but tomorrow – who can say where it will end up? (*holds it to his eye*) Maybe it will turn into the Master's eyes! (*holds it to his chest*) Or maybe his heart! (*holds it behind himself*) Or maybe it'll become his ... who knows! Who can say which bit of food will lodge in what part of the body that eats it? (*chuckles*)

No one can say! Just like no one can guess what I do with this food before I cook it, or what I think of while I am cooking it. But the fact remains: the food I touch today, turns into my masters' bodies tomorrow.

See this onion? When I peel it, (*as he begins to peel it*) I think of the Young Madam ... it doesn't matter which one – the youngest one in the house. I think I am slooowly peeling off her clothes, carefully ... Yes. Mustn't hurt her! Mustn't make her cry! Until they're all off ... every last little bit of clinging cloth ... until there it is at last, white, perfect ... shining (*holds it to his nose, inhaling deeply*) Smelling powerfully! Ahhhh ... (*licking the onion*) let me lick it a bit, let me share her ... future! (*bites the onion*) taste her ... spice! Yes! That is good. (*chuckles*)

Then I put it down on my chopping board and – (*chops neatly and quickly*) what am I cutting? Could it be ... some part of the Master's round, perfect, pearl-like ... *treasures*? Yes! I think it could be! Yes! I slice them up into tiny little pieces – yes, my eyes fill with tears, to imagine the pain – yes, I smile to imagine his anger, if he knew what I was doing with his future body – I laugh, because he will never know. Even if he guesses ... he will never KNOW.

Picks up a head of garlic.

And these cloves of garlic, what will they become? How hard they are, how succulent they taste! Yes – yes – I put each one in my mouth, before I crush it with the side of my knife and throw it into the pan –

And these tomatoes too – and these chillies – yes, I taste everything, bite everything, smell everything. Then I throw it into the pan and the hot oil burns away all impurities, and fries away my thoughts, my feelings, my desires.

Yes. I remove all trace of my today, until all that remains is the taste of my Master's tomorrow.

Because what is a servant? You might think he is a cook, or a sweeper or a clothes' washer. But I will tell you what he is: a timekeeper. I save time for my masters. I store it along the edge of my knife, in the tips of my fingers and in the hours of my life. But I am old now and soon to die. So you have come. They need someone new and fresh from whom to squeeze out the days and weeks and years of their lives. Yes.

So you have come. You are waiting to hear my advice.

Here it is now: keep your lid tightly shut, or you will lose your flavour. Don't lose the keys to your mind, or you will lose your job. Don't use your Master's time to fill your purse or you will lose your life.

And that is all you need to know.

Curtain.

THE DHOBI'S WIFE

The DHOBI'S WIFE is a middle-aged woman. She is dressed neatly and her manner is extremely submissive. She addresses all her remarks to an unseen police inspector.

DHOBI'S WIFE:

Inspector? Please, my husband ... he is here? Sir, please! I can explain (*flinches*) - please, wait! Let me explain - he did nothing! He - no (*as if warding off blows*) - just listen to me one minute - the old man was already dead! (*wards of a blow*) No, sir, no - not cheeky ... please listen to me ... it's the clothes, sir - the clothes ... the old man was wearing the wrong clothes when he died! (*stands a little straighter*)

Yes sir, yes - of course I'm sure! We're the ones who wash the clothes, aren't we? So we know, don't we? We notice when there's a change in a household's routines. Two months ago, that's when we began to notice the changes. Small changes - a stain here, a mark there, still, we see them, we notice them. But that very morning, when I helped my husband count the clothes I said, *See? There is something strange here ... two sets of clothes for the Old Man ...* That's how they came to us. Two sets of clothes.

Sir, please listen to me: every Sunday, my husband collects the clothes to wash for the week, and at the same time he delivers the last week's clothes. You must be knowing how it is! In all big houses it is the same. This week also he went. To the top floor. That's where the old man lives ... used to live. On the ground floor there's an office. On Sundays that place is empty. One *gurkha* sits there, to guard the lift. There is only this lift to go up, no stairs, not in front. In the back there are stairs, but we come by the front.

My husband takes his bundle to the top floor. Like every Sunday, he goes upstairs in the lift. He rings the doorbell. But no one comes. So he tries the door - and it is open.

Every Sunday he does the same thing – first he rings the bell, then he tries the door. Many times it is open. There is no other way to enter the house, after all. They might as well keep it open.

In front of the lift is a big room. Many times the Old Man is there, taking tea. Today, the Old Man is not there. No one is there, in the front room.

My husband puts his bundle on the floor. He starts to open it. Still no one has come. No *bai*, no cook, nobody. Maybe they are all watching TV? He does not mind. Someone will come. After all, the door was open. Somebody is in the house. He has rung the bell. Somebody will come.

So he puts the clothes out in order: first the small pieces, then the big ones. Eight bed sheets, four pillowcases – small, four pillowcases – big. Bedspreads, two. Four towels – big. Sixteen towels – small. Coloured hand towels, eight. Bathmats, eight. No, sir, no! I must tell you everything! This is how you will see why I know what I know! Napkins – small, fourteen. Napkins – big, white, twelve. Napkins – big, coloured, seventeen – they had a party – you see? Or else, why so many mouth-wipe cloths? In this house, the coloured mouth-wipe comes out only for a party. Other times, simple white. Same for towels. See the hand towels? Coloured. That's how I know. When the guests come in, the hand towels come out! Kitchen towels, twenty. That shows it's a dinner. If it's a lunch, kitchen towels are less. I don't know why, but that's how it is.

Anyway. So, then the clothes. Not many clothes from this household. After all, the Old Man lives – ah, again! – *used to live* – alone with his eldest daughter. Unmarried, she. Something wrong there ... poor thing. Anyway, she wears only simple cotton saris. Plain coloured, light starch. Changes twice a day – so 14 saris every week, 14 blouses, 7 petticoats – see! She changes the blouse and the sari but not the petticoat! Now here is another thing: she does not send us her small clothes – the underwear. Who can say why? Maybe she washes them herself, by hand. Some ladies are like that. Even the unmarried ones. Proud about their small clothes.

But whatever she hides underneath, above she wears only the plainest of the plain. Even for the party – nothing special – or anyway, if she wears something special, she doesn't send it to us for a wash! Never anything brightly coloured, that's for sure – nothing I have seen, nothing from her is bright-coloured. Oh, and housecoat, one. She has six and she changes them once every week, each week different.

So far, completely normal.

But then we come to the Old Man's clothes. See, we have been washing for that household maybe ten-twelve years. The same clothes every day, for ten-twelve years – meaning: week after week, the same routine, the same clothes.

Of course, now and then there are a few changes – something gets torn, something gets stained, something gets thrown away – but even those changes, after ten-twelve years, we get used to them.

For instance, twice a year – once at Diwali, once for his birthday – the Old Man gets something new. Always, it is the same thing: white kurta, with chikan embroidery and white cotton pyjamas. Inside he wears one vest and of course, underneath, one underpant. At night he wears foreign pantsuit, dark colours, hand wash, cold water, no starch. Each week, one pantsuit. Last week, it was the dark blue with red design (*she gestures*) at the neck, the cuffs.

His daughter, poor thing, her saris may come and go. God knows her father has enough money to buy her a thousand saris every day, but year in, year out, the same thing, the same thing.

That's what we have been seeing. For ten years.

But this week it was different. You think we won't notice? One extra mulmul kurta and pyjama! Now: what could that mean? Of course - I am not saying there is never any change! One time the Old Man was sick, he was in hospital and then - for a month? Nothing! For two months? Nothing! All was being washed in the hospital or - maybe, who knows, I never asked - maybe he wore something else. I can't say. All I can say is, for two months, we did not wash the Old Man's clothes.

And sometimes he has been a little feverish, then he lies in bed all day and he doesn't get out of his foreign pantsuit. So then there are less mulmul kurtas to wash, less white pyjamas. One week, I remember, there was only one set: and I asked my husband, "The Old Man, is he well? What is the matter with him? Will he ever get out of bed?" But by next Sunday, back he was, with fourteen sets, bathing twice a day, changing twice a day – I can smell the powder! That's how I know!

But this week, this week ... so strange! One extra kurta and pyjama! When a man is ill, he will use one less set, two less sets ... but when will he use one EXTRA set? When he already changes twice a day? And another strange thing. One of the sets was new. Yes. Unused. That's what we saw - it was still as fresh as the day it came from the shop. I checked for pins - sometimes there are pins and they can tear the cloth and then we get blamed. So I checked, when I saw that it was something new and unused - and sure enough, there was a pin! I took it out. I can show it to you, if you want ...

Okay, okay ... where was I? My husband was counting the clothes. He was putting them side by side - each set of washed, ironed clothes. There were ... (*quick mental count*) nine sets in all - and usually, by the time he does that, someone is there to check the clothes. To see that he has brought everything back.

But today there was no one.

He still has one other household to visit. What should he do?

He waited. He listened for sounds. Then he waited again. Still there was no one. He stood up. He got a little scared. There were no sounds anywhere. He came down in the lift. He saw the *gurkha*. He said, "I have forgotten one thing, it is with my wife but I have left the balance clothes upstairs. Please, in three minutes I will come back. The *gurkha* said, "Go, go." Ask him, he'll tell you, what I am saying is true.

My husband told me what he had seen. First I shouted at him, "You left the clothes! You got no payment? No return clothes? Have you gone mad?"

But he said to me, "Listen, something is wrong in that house. And I am alone there. Who can say what will happen next?" Then, he went back again!

She stops. She looks around.

Now. This is what I know for sure. The rest ... you tell me?

He went back there – the next thing I hear, everyone is saying, he killed the Old Man. He found the body, alone in the house. And you say he is the one who found the body. And he was alone in the house. But I say ... something was wrong in that house from before! Check the clothes! Ask them what they saw! Ask them who they saw!

She becomes agitated. She speaks in a louder voice, as if her audience is moving away from her.

Sir, sir – please! Won't you listen to me, sir – please! The extra clothes, sir – don't you see? Someone has planned something. And they needed to change his clothes before the body was found – so they got a new set and they gave it to us to wash – no sir, please! You listen to what I am saying – ask someone in the house – the maid, the cook – someone! You will find one extra kurta-pyjama – and on that will be your answer –

Lights fade out. Curtain.

LADIES' NIGHT

Characters

YOUTH

An unnamed young man of indeterminate age and class. His appearance suggests a meek, unambitious personality, the only son of middle-aged, middle-salaried parents. He is painfully thin, wears his shirt tucked in and carries a black plastic folder under his arm. His pants are plain and black, his shirt is brown and white. Please also see the endnote for more details/suggestions.

GROUP

Eight to ten young women of varying sizes and shapes. They are dressed in a single colour – not uniform in shade or fashion – yet similar enough to see that it's clearly not by chance. If they wear white, for instance, then it should not be a uniform white, but varying levels and textures of whiteness – such as khadi and chiffon, poplin and chikan, bleached and unbleached. Regardless of whether they wear Western or Indian clothes, they are wholly covered, with only their faces bare (bare in the sense visible) but covered in make-up. The make-up is highly distinctive, like a mask: stark white skin, with staring eyes outlined in bright red, such that even when they shut their eyes, their eyelids have the image of open, staring eyes painted on. No eyebrows. Bright red mouths in a Kathakali dancer's fixed stylized smile. They wear identical shaggy wigs, the hair wild and knotted.

GODDESS

Similar to the rest of the group except that she has a more classical dress and style – something between Bharatanatyam and Kathakali – with either a fan in front or the stiff skirt. She must look huge and imposing. She wears a crown of winking lights and has an extra pair of (cardboard) arms raised up behind her. There's a lightning bolt in one hand and a meat cleaver in the other.

Late night, a deserted bus stop on a darkened street. In the backdrop, a city's tall buildings in silhouette. Overhead, a full moon. YOUTH is at a bus stop, alone, and half perched on the horizontal bar.

SFX: The continuous rumble of traffic in the distance.

YOUTH: Some nights ago. I was standing at a bus stop. This bus stop. It was late. Only one street light was working. I heard a sound ...

SFX: Running footsteps approaching from stage right, a man's slippered feet (not sneakers or boots), passing across the front of the stage and onwards, out the left. The sound has an echoing quality, a reverb effect, suggesting an element of something weird and unexpected though NOT supernatural.

YOUTH: A man came running towards me –

SFX: Heavy panting and an incoherent shout, followed immediately by the sounds of more running feet.

YOUTH: I called after him, "What? What?" – but more men came running, passing me, some saying –

SFX: Variously, in Hindi/English "Watch out, watch out! They're coming, they're coming – save yourself, you fool – you moron – you imbecile – it's Ladies' Night – IT'S LADIES' NIGHT!" The sounds pass away to the left.

YOUTH: (*calls after the voices*) What? Who? Stop – stop – I didn't understand – what is Ladies' Night?

(*to the audience once more*) I don't know what is "Ladies' Night". Maybe something to do with the moon? It is going to be full tonight, that much I know.

But none of them stop. I look around. I can see nothing. It is time for the bus. And anyway, where can I go? My home is far away. My mother stays up, waiting till I get back. She will not eat until after I eat.

SFX: From stage left, the sound of an approaching vehicle.

YOUTH: Ah! The bus is coming! (*he straightens up, leaning out in that expectant way. Lights shine in his face from stage left, in the manner of approaching headlights. He shades his eyes, steps forward, holds up his arm, waves enthusiastically)*

SFX: The sound of a horn, impatient, like that of a driver who is signalling that he will not stop. The ting-ting sound of the bus conductor signalling to move on. The sounds approach from the left, pass in front of the YOUTH, then recede into the distance, stage right.

YOUTH: (*his shoulders slump, as the lights pass in front and then away from him*) Ahh! It doesn't stop. This is the problem with this area. The buses are full when they leave the terminal. They don't like to stop until they've gone two stops away. (*he returns to his seat on the bar*)

But the next bus will come in forty minutes. I know I will have a better chance. I have been walking in the sun all day. Four job interviews. One packet of bhujia for lunch. Two soft drinks. They cost a lot, those soft drinks.

It's very quiet. It's very hot. It's very still. (*he looks around*)

Then I hear a sound. I *think* I hear a sound. First one side. Then the other. I see nothing. But it begins to grow ...

SFX: A rustling sound, similar to the wind stirring up dry leaves except that it escalates quickly, its source invisible until –

The GROUP appears out of the darkness, giving the impression of swooping, though they are not running. They are the source of the sound, though it isn't immediately obvious how they are making it. The only source of light is the single street lamp across the street from the bus stop, so they are not easy to see. It isn't clear how many there are, or what/who they are. At the time of their approach, they are swathed in black.

They are carrying sheets of red cellophane paper in their hands, waving it in the air around them as they approach.

One of them, having thrown back her outer sheath of black, enters the bus shelter. Stops when she sees YOUTH, then comes under the canopy and takes her place on the bar. She sits as far from him as she can.

YOUTH: Then, a girl is ... there. I do not see her come. Just suddenly, she is ... there.

She is sitting far from me.

All the time, there is a sound. All around. (*he glances on either side, but in the manner of someone who does not want to see anything. Then he flinches*) Ah! There! Is that? (*calls out*) Ho! Is there someone there?

The moment he has turned away from her GIRL 1 slides along the bar, towards YOUTH. She is perhaps three spaces distant from where he is perched, which is at the stage left end of the bar, but not at its absolute end. He has left a single-person space between himself and the absolute end.

(*when he turns back around, he sees that GIRL 1 has moved*)

Naturally, I do not look directly at this girl. Or lady I should say. I don't want to turn and look at her, because maybe she will feel ... uncomfortable. After all, I am a man. And she is a girl! Alone, on the street! Late at night! She will be afraid of me, na? Of course she will. I want to tell her not to worry. Because she's safe with me. I will never hurt a woman.

Still, even from the corner of my eye I can see there's something strange about her –

While he talks, one of the GROUP sidles up behind him, to his left (i.e. the audience's right), careful to remain perfectly quiet until the moment when she crackles her paper right behind his head.

YOUTH: AH! Who – what – ! (*swinging around*)

There's no one there; but when he returns to his initial position GIRL 2 is also under the canopy, seated on his right. Like GIRL 1, she looks straight ahead, not at him. He immediately flinches and slides sideways, along the rail, to his left. This of course brings him closer to GIRL 1. But there is still some space between them.

YOUTH: It's very late at night. After ten o'clock. I want to tell these girls – I think they are girls, not ladies, because they have left their hair open – that they must not be out late at night. It is not safe.

GIRL 3 now enters the shelter, on the YOUTH's left and joins GIRL 1 who shifts her position up a notch so that she is now only a half space away from him. Ultimately, six girls will be perched alongside YOUTH on the bar, with him in the centre, a half space on either side. He continues talking, each time taking breaks to jump and turn around in response to the rustling of paper.

There are a lot of bad men in the city. They do not show any respect to girls. It is a great shame. After all, in our culture, we are brought up to think of all girls as our sisters. *Ah!* What was that? What WAS THAT? We must show them respect. They are girls after all. One day they will be mothers.

GIRL 4 settles in.

At the same time, I must admit, modern girls these days do not know how to behave. They are learning some Very Bad Habits. From the films and from the TV and from the Western Foreigners. Look at how they dress? (*clicks his tongue*) tch-tch-tch! It makes me very sad to see them with their little-little skirts and their tight-tight jeans ... very sad. And the sari *blouse* - uh! Tight like anything. *Wait – who was that – what* – It makes me sick to see girls from good families walking around so exposed.

GIRL 5 arrives.

Some of my friends, they say: we will respect girls if they behave in the right way. But when they behave in the wrong way, then why should we respect them? After all, respect must be earned. It does not come free of charge. *Ha! I saw you – who are you – what?* Like pet dogs, when you have a pet dog in the house, it is clean and well fed, nicely behaved, that is one thing. We respect that doggie. But the bitch on the street? Anyone can kick her or beat her, it doesn't matter. She is for all to use and abuse.

GIRL 6 takes her place. The moment GIRL 2 shifts up a notch towards him, YOUTH jerks forward, moving out from under the canopy and away from the bar altogether while continuing to talk.

Who are these girls? Why are they out so late? Now I

remember. I read something. About Ladies' Night. On full moons. I feel I should talk to them. But they won't listen. Girls don't listen these days.

While YOUTH continues to talk to the audience, the GROUP begins to move now as a group. Their movements are at all times deliberate and stylized, but never hesitant.

They surround YOUTH, back and sides, leaving him free to move forward.

They don't touch YOUTH right away. They start by merely threatening to touch him, to which he reacts by contorting his body away from their hands while making brief fluting cries.

YOUTH: (*for the first time, he addresses them directly*) I am not a bad man, you see. Not like the others. I will never hurt a girl. Why, I would never dream of hurting a girl. *Oo!* Never even touch them on the bus or anything. It's wrong to do such things – *ah!* – Even though I have friends who do it. They think it's – *ah!* – what girls want – *no!* – a way of showing appreciation, because – *ah!* – otherwise, otherwise – *ee!* – why do girls bother to wear pretty clothes? And paint their faces? Or – *ooh!* – or ...

Now they start to lay their hands on him. It begins as a light plucking motion, as if they are picking lint off his clothes but his attempts to brush off the hands results in their redoubling their efforts.

YOUTH: Listen – please! – listen to me! I have never done anything to any girl. Really. Never. Not even looked at naked pictures. On the Internet. Never. I swear on my mother – I have the greatest respect –

Now they have him in their grip. There's no denying it any more. He makes feeble attempts to struggle, but there's no question of his succeeding. Partly supporting him, they push/pull him forward, while behind them, two of the GIRLs shift the bus shelter out of the way. It should not look like they are actually shifting it, but that they are moving him from behind it, away from the road – without actually moving him from centre stage. The light shifts from the semi-realism of the street lamp, directly in front, to the cold blue light of the moon overhead and then to semi-fanciful effects, to suit the mood of the situation.

SFX: Rhythmic, portentous music. Not especially melodic, but not ugly either.

YOUTH: What have I done wrong? Nothing! I have never done anything to any girl. Really. Never. Not even looked at a picture of a girl. On the Internet. Never. I swear on my mother – I have the greatest respect –

They wrap him tight in bright red cloth. This manoeuvre must be managed with neat precision regardless of his resistance with the GIRLs working in unison, in matched pairs on either side of YOUTH. The cloth can be a single vast swaddling sheet or else broad strips that they use to wrap him up tight – like a mummy but in red – leaving only his face free with the rest of his head securely wrapped. Whatever method they use, it must be quick and the end result should be that he looks like a corpse.

YOUTH: (*his voice begins to break into sobs during this passage. He repeats himself, he begs, he pleads*) What are you doing? No don't – I can't be treated like this. Don't, please – don't hurt me – please! What are you going to do? Are you going to ... to ... kill me? Just like that? For no reason? But, but, WHY? Why ME? What've I done to you, or to anyone? I ... I'm not bad, I've not hurt anyone – please! Oh! Oh! No – no – don't do this, don't, don't – please! I'm begging you now – please! Just tell me what you're doing! I'm a good boy – my mother's going to be so worried – don't you care about what another woman feels? She'll be crying and praying, if I don't come home – I could be your brother – your father – your uncle – oh *PLEASE!* Just LEAVE ME ... Just let me go ... I won't tell anyone – I'll ... never tell ... What are you – why are you – who ... what ... PLEASE. Don't hurt me. I swear to you, I'll never hurt anyone, any girl, any woman ever again – EVER, NEVER, NEVERNEVERNEVER ... (*sobs*) I swear, I swear, I swear, never, ever ... (*sobs*)

As soon as they are done, the mood shifts and they stretch him out on the floor, but raised up slightly, perhaps a foot or so above the stage floor, as if he's on a corpse bier. The audience should be able to see him easily. As they lay him out, the

GODDESS comes forward into view. She has been lurking all along, glittering quietly without revealing herself.

YOUTH: What's happening – what – are you going to just leave me here? What are you doing – no, please no – *Uhhhh* –

The GODDESS places her foot on him.

GODDESS: HUSH!

SFX: Drumming begins. It is the hard, brash drum of the Ganesh festival.

GIRLS: (*in chorus*) HUSHHHHHHHHHHHHH!

GODDESS: (*she sings/intones, with a catchy, rap music cadence, the music supporting her*) I am the Goddess WITH NO NAME.

I am the Goddess of RAPE AND SHAME.

Those who see me WILL REGRET.

Their crimes of LUST and GENDERED PAIN.

She dances, as the GIRLs take up her chant. Her dance is from side to side, with broad powerful movements, springing from one foot to the other.

ANY ONE, of *ANY* FAITH

ANY RACE and *ANY* AGE

ANY PLACE and *ANY* CREED

Can call to me

In time of NEED!

GIRLS: I am the Goddess WITH NO NAME!

I am the Goddess of RAPE AND SHAME!

Those who see me WILL REGRET!

Their crimes of LUST and GENDERED PAIN!

Each repetition is faster than the one before, ending with the third repetition and a loud final BANG from the drum.

GODDESS: (*holding her hand up for silence*) So! Youth. Foolish, stupid boy. Who told you to come out on the streets on Ladies'

Night? Who told you to stand alone and unprotected in a deserted place? Who told you to wear black pants and a white shirt? For all these foolish, thoughtless errors, you are being PUNISHED. Today, you have been CHOSEN. To represent ALL THOSE MEN who harm GIRLS and WOMEN and CHILDREN for NO REASON AT ALL.

YOUTH: No – no! Please! I've done nothing, nothing at all –

GODDESS: (*digs her foot into him*) HUSH!

GIRLS: HUSHHHH!

GODDESS: Our PARENTS cannot protect us! The POLICE cannot protect us! The POLITICIANS cannot protect us! So we have gone to a HIGHER AUTHORITY! We have created a GODDESS TO PROTECT US. Yes! Our own GODDESS WITH NO NAME.

GIRLS: (*murmuring chorus*) Goddess With No Name – Goddess of Rape and Shame ... (*they keep up a continuous murmuring hum*) ... Those Who See Me Will Regret ... Their Crimes of Lust and Gendered Pain ...

YOUTH: Please – please! Forgive me, forgive me. Let me go – I haven't – I won't –

GODDESS: Hush. Tell me, youth: how shall we punish you for the crimes that others have committed against girls, women and children?

YOUTH: Let me go. Please. I'll never do it again – I'll never do anything again – I'll be quiet – I'll be kind – I'll be good –

GODDESS: I'll tell you what we won't do: we won't shove rods in your anus; we won't pour acid on your balls; we won't pluck out your eyes.

YOUTH: N-n-n-no! PLEASE! No. Not that. Not m-m-my eyes. Or m-m-my – b-b-b-b –

GODDESS: We won't set you on fire. We won't cut off your penis. We won't tear out your entrails. No. We won't do any of those things.

YOUTH: P-p-p-p-lease ... please. I'll do whatever you want. Whatever you tell me. Please. Please. Just. Let. Me. G-g-g-g-go ...

GODDESS: We'll let you go.

YOUTH: P-p-p-p-lease ... please ... please ... please ...

GODDESS: We'll let you go on, we'll let you live the rest of your life, remembering this night. Because you will, won't you? Ladies' Night. Every full moon night. You'll remember being powerless and helpless and frightened. You'll remember being tied up like a corpse. You'll remember shitting your pants. You'll remember knowing that your life will never be the same. You'll never get married. You'll never have children. Your penis will shrivel up and fall off. You'll die with the sound of my voice in year ears. The voice of the Goddess With No Name. The Goddess of Rape and Shame.

She straightens up.

And that is all. For tonight. Come, my girls. Let's go. We've done our job. For tonight.

She begins a sideways movement towards stage left that will take her out of view, while facing the audience.

GIRLS: (*subdued and calm as they surround the GODDESS, leaving as a flock. They continue chanting till the last one has gone*) For tonight. For tonight. For tonight. For tonight. For tonight ...

Silence envelops the stage. All other lights fade away until there's only a single spotlight, bearing down on YOUTH's face, still obscured with the red bandages. Only his mouth moves.

YOUTH: (*dry sob*) And that's how they left me. Tied up like a corpse. And I'll never know why. Why me. Why me.

Why. Me.

Why. Why. Why.

Cut to black. Curtain.

ENDNOTE

1. In my view, the role of YOUTH must be played by a young woman. I have two reasons for preferring this. I think it would be strangely empowering for the girl who takes that role – to be the oppressed character in the persona of a man. By contrast, for any young man, particularly one who is NOT a professional actor, the experience of being tied up in red winding cloths by a group of girls might be deeply unpleasant.

2. Meanwhile, the roles of the GROUP might be played by men and women. We never see their actual faces or figures. Once again, I think it would be empowering for both men and women to play these roles interchangeably – except for the GODDESS, since she is the only one who speaks rather than chants.

THE RAPE ARTIST

A Dramatic Dialogue

Characters

NIMMI

The host of the show, a glamorous/attractive middle-aged woman.

BUNTY

A young man, noticeably thin and weedy. He wears very tight jeans, a flashy shirt, a big watch, pointy shoes.

The stage is set up as if for a TV interview on a set that pretends to be a drawing room. NIMMI and BUNTY are both already seated.

SFX: Applause as scene begins.

NIMMI: Thank you for joining us tonight! I'd like to introduce our guest for the evening ... Mr Bunty! (*turns to BUNTY*) Hello, Mr Bunty! Or, as you prefer to be known, Mr Rape Artist. Tell our viewers, Mr Bunty, what is it you do?

BUNTY: Uhh ... as my title says, I'm a ... uhh ... Rape Artist.

NIMMI: If you don't mind me saying so, Mr Bunty, that's an extremely *unusual* profession –

BUNTY: Why should I mind? After all, it's true. In fact, I think I am the first one to invent this art.

NIMMI: Really? But –

BUNTY: (*cutting in*) I am talking about the *art* of rape. Not the *crime*.

NIMMI: Yes, that's what you said at the time of your interview. Frankly, Mr Bunty, it's hard to understand the difference between the two. But you assured us there IS a difference. Can you explain?

BUNTY: Well, the crime of rape is what anyone can do – that is, for instance, a man can force a woman to ... you know ... (*clears his throat*)

NIMMI: ... have intercourse with him. So where is the art in that? It's just a terrible, horrific crime –

SFX: Applause.

– that we condemn in the strongest possible terms.

BUNTY: Uhh ...

NIMMI: (*facing towards the audience. This is clearly her mission statement*) In fact, many of us believe the only solution for rape is to burn the convicted rapist in public and castrate his father, brothers, uncles and sons.

SFX: Roars and cheers.

BUNTY: Uhhh ...

NIMMI: *All* the male blood relatives of a rapist should suffer along with him for the crime of trampling on a woman's honour!

SFX: Roars and cheers.

BUNTY: (*he has been making quelling gestures*) Uhhh ... But that's not what I am talking about. That's just rape. Not the *art* of rape. When something is an Art, it means it's *not* the thing that's being ... you know ... I mean, a portrait of someone is Art, because it looks like the person without *being* the person.

NIMMI: Oh! So you mean you've found a way of ... of ... creating artificial rapes?

BUNTY: No, that's not it. After all, a portrait isn't "artificial" it's ... a ... uhh ...

NIMMI: Representation. I get you. But I still don't understand how ...?

BUNTY: I can demonstrate in just a couple of minutes.

NIMMI: Go ahead.

BUNTY: So ... I'll be demonstrating on you?

NIMMI: (*she nods*) Yes, yes. Go ahead.

BUNTY: Sure you won't mind?

NIMMI: You told us at the interview that you wouldn't ... I mean, there's no physical action involved –

BUNTY: Correct. But it's still, I mean ... you might find yourself feeling ... a bit ... you know ... *violated* at the end of it.

NIMMI: I don't understand how that's possible, so I ... (*smiles indulgently*) I'm willing to take the risk.

BUNTY: Basically, it's just one question. Shall I start?

NIMMI: Yes! Go ahead.

BUNTY: Okay, here's the question: May I rape you?

NIMMI: (*glances at the audience in amused disbelief*) Huh – what do you mean! How can I –

BUNTY: (*cutting in*) Please. Just answer the question. I'll ask it again: May I rape you?

NIMMI: No! Of course NOT! Why should I –

BUNTY: (*cutting in*) Fine! In that case, I *will* rape you.

Brief silence during which BUNTY contemplates his nails.

NIMMI: (*puzzled, slightly irritated*) I ... I don't understand. What have you demonstrated?

BUNTY: That you want to get raped.

NIMMI: But I said ...

BUNTY: (*not looking up*) You want to be raped now?

NIMMI: I already said, *no*! Of course not. No one can "want" to be raped. It is, by definition, something that cannot be wanted! How can you even ask the question?

BUNTY: So that was a "no"?

NIMMI: Yes, it was a "no".

BUNTY: Hmmm! Confusing! I mean, are you saying "yes" or "no"?

NIMMI: No!

BUNTY: Meaning you're not saying "no"?

NIMMI: You know what I'm saying! I said "no" and only "no".

BUNTY: That's not true! A moment back, you said "yes" –

NIMMI: I said "yes" in answer to your question about whether or not I said "no"! You're deliberately confusing the issue –

BUNTY: Of course I am. It's part of my act. So back to the question. May I rape you, yes or no?

NIMMI: No. Like I said the first time. No.

BUNTY: And "no" means "no", right?

NIMMI: Right.

BUNTY: (*he is starting to look triumphant*) Except that, for a rapist it actually means "yes" –

NIMMI: It does not. "No" never means "yes" –

BUNTY: It does. When it comes to rape.

NIMMI: NO!

BUNTY: Let me demonstrate, again: Shall I rape you?

NIMMI: NO! NO! A million times NO!

Pause.

BUNTY: So then ... I will. (*he sits forward, energized*) You don't understand what I'm saying, do you? (*he doesn't wait for a *response. He stands up and walks around, gesturing as he speaks)* No, of course you don't. So I'll explain.

Rape is defined in the negative – you said so yourself. It's an act that *cannot* be wanted. Which is all very well, as definitions go. It seems so simple, so clear. When a man wants to have sex and when a woman says "no", it means he must go away without having sex.

This is all very well except ... except for a man who *wants* to commit rape. That is, someone who *enjoys* forcing himself on women. Someone who adores the resistance, the chase, the conquest.

Granted, not all men are like that.

But when we talk about a man who *is* like that, a man who gets pleasure by forcing his sexual attention upon women who resist him ... (*turns with a triumphant expression*) Well, then!

NIMMI: Well, then – what?

BUNTY: He realizes that he's a fish in the water – a grasshopper in grass – a bird in the sky!

Because as a rapist, he's in the best of all possible worlds!

Why? Ask me, why.

NIMMI: (*frowning*) All right, why?

BUNTY: *Because all women, everywhere, are trained to resist him!*

Do you see my point?

NIMMI: No, not really –

BUNTY: By saying "no" to rape, women are in effect being trained to say "yes" to a rapist – *because "no" is what he wants to hear!* In short, women are trained to enable a rapist to be a rapist by ... (*he looks expectantly in her direction, encouraging her with hand gestures to complete his statement*)

NIMMI: ... not wanting to be raped. (*she looks confused as well as glum*)

SFX: Applause.

BUNTY: (*he is delighted with himself*) Pretty good, huh?

NIMMI: No, awful. (*she touches her forehead*) You're messing with my brain.

BUNTY: Heh! Yep. I warned you about that. You didn't believe that I could do it, but I've just demonstrated a Super Deluxe Mind Foggle.

NIMMI: Foggle?

BUNTY: I forced a thought into your brain without your permission. I dumped my load of hot, steaming, ideas straight into your quivering, defenceless, submissive brain! And now I'm in there, all my little wrigglers, swarming through your thoughts, merging with your memories until you'll never be able to dig me out of there. And all at a distance, without the slightest touch!

SFX: Applause.

NIMMI: Sick. You're very sick.

BUNTY: It takes skill to do what I just did. That's why I call myself a rape *artist*. Admit it, you've never had this happen to you before.

NIMMI: It's wrong. It's an assault.

BUNTY: Best of all, no laws can stop me! Come on. Shall I do it again?

NIMMI: No!

BUNTY: Please! I'll never get a chance like this again – to perform live on TV!

NIMMI: No –

BUNTY: But your viewers WANT to see me do it again!

NIMMI: No, they *don't*!

BUNTY: You heard them – they were applauding –

NIMMI: No, no – you can see there's no studio audience – someone must have turned on the applause track by mistake.

SFX: Applause.

BUNTY: Anyway, it doesn't matter. Because people are hypocrites. Society "condemns" rape – on all the TV panels that's what everyone says. But in private? In the secret toilets of their minds? People *love* rape. Not just men – women too!

NIMMI: That is a complete and horrible LIE –

BUNTY: No, it's not. Rape makes men feel powerful and women feel virtuous.

NIMMI: What are you *saying*!

BUNTY: Only a virtuous woman can claim to be raped, right?

NIMMI: No!

BUNTY: (*carrying on regardless*) So. Work the equation backwards: if a woman can prove she's been raped, it *has* to mean she was virtuous!

NIMMI: But who says only a virtuous woman can claim to be raped?

BUNTY: Ask anyone, anywhere – on the streets, in the shops, in homes everywhere – they'll tell you what everyone knows. (*he shrugs and shakes his head*)

NIMMI: Which is?

BUNTY: That a woman with no virtue is like a house with no doors: easily looted.

NIMMI: But virtue isn't a lootable asset like ... like ... jewellery or paintings –

BUNTY: (*shrugs*) You asked me to tell you what people say.

NIMMI: And anyway, I've never heard anyone say that. Certainly not any women.

BUNTY: All right, then, what about *Gone with the Wind*?

NIMMI: (*nonplussed*) You mean, the American Civil War classic?

BUNTY: Yes, yes – well, the movie anyway. I've only seen the movie. Only that one scene, in fact.

NIMMI: What scene?

BUNTY: You know perfectly well. I've watched it a thousand times on YouTube. Bet you have too. The scene in which Clark Gable drags Vivian Leigh to the bedroom, followed by silence. Because for the first time in her life, she gets nailed good and proper.

NIMMI: It's JUST A MOVIE! Not a documentary!

BUNTY: But it demonstrates my point perfectly: that women are lying when they say they don't enjoy rape. Yes, it's "only a movie", it's "only fiction", blah-blah-blah. But it's a fiction that's repeated again and again – in movies, in Mills & Boon, on TV. It's the kind of fiction that women watch and read and enjoy again and again.

SFX: Applause.

NIMMI: What about the laws, then?

BUNTY: All these fictions make the same point: that when women want to get raped, they say NO – which is how they get raped – and that's also when they really enjoy sex – that's when they have their first ... you know ... *whatever*. It's all there in *Gone with the Wind*! And in Mills & Boon! Coz it's a fact of nature! Get over it.

SFX: Applause.

NIMMI: So why do courts punish convicted rapists? If society secretly "loves" rape?

BUNTY: Because impotent old men make laws to curb the natural appetites of young people –

NIMMI: (*she shakes her head*) No, no, NO!

BUNTY: – after all, it takes two to create a rape: a rapist who wants to force his attentions on a woman and a woman who is willing to resist him! Unless she resists him, she won't get raped – and if she can't get raped, she won't enjoy sex –

SFX: Applause.

NIMMI: Stop – *stop!* (*holding her head*) It's illegal to even *think* such thoughts!

BUNTY: So anyway. Back to my question. May I ask it again?

NIMMI: (*shaking her head*) No, I ... (*stops*) Wait. Let me think this through ...

BUNTY: What?

NIMMI: Your question. I'm starting to see a way through the maze. Okay. Ask me again?

BUNTY: Now you *want* me to ask it?

NIMMI: Yes.

BUNTY: You're sure?

NIMMI: Yes.

BUNTY: (*slightly uncertain*) All right. Okay. (*clears throat*) Shall I rape you?

NIMMI: (*leaning forward, looking intense*) What ... what happens if I say "yes"?

BUNTY: Just answer the question.

NIMMI: But if I say "yes" ... I mean, what happens if I say "yes"?

BUNTY: (*shrugs*) You won't know unless you try it.

NIMMI: All right, then. I ... I'll say "yes" – but only to see where this goes –

BUNTY: Uh-uh. Sorry. If that's a "yes" with quotation marks, then it doesn't count.

NIMMI: Okay. Okay. Then it's a full and complete YES. No quotation marks.

BUNTY: Sorry, but I don't believe you.

NIMMI: You heard me.

BUNTY: I don't believe you.

NIMMI: What do you want me to do?

BUNTY: You know perfectly well what I mean. *Just say the words!*

NIMMI: (*squaring her shoulders, a couple of false starts*) Okay! I ... want ... you ... to ... (*falters*) to ... (*stops, dismayed*) No! I can't. I just *can't* say it.

SFX: Applause.

BUNTY: (*grins*) I know! That's what's so amazing! It's like every woman is programmed to give the rapist exactly what he wants! By maintaining this ready-made switch inside her head that makes her incapable of saying the one thing that might ... well ... (*he stops suddenly and shrugs*).

NIMMI: Well, what?

BUNTY: I mean, it's not for *me* to say.

NIMMI: No, go *on* – I think we're finally getting somewhere –

BUNTY: No. Why should I? After all, it's not my problem that women have this switch – in fact, it's because of the switch that I can be an Artist.

NIMMI: All right, if you won't ask me, then I'll go one step further and demand that you ... that you rape me. There. I said it.

BUNTY: But you didn't mean it.

NIMMI: You heard me! I'm demanding – no, *ordering* you! – to rape me!

BUNTY: (*shrugs*) You said yourself just five minutes ago – it's not possible to want something that can't be wanted –

NIMMI: But according to you, the only correct response to a rapist is to say "yes' to him?

BUNTY: Sure. Except that he'll hear no either way.

NIMMI: Meaning, he'll rape me, regardless of what I say.

BUNTY: Of course. He's a rapist. You can't want what he wants.

NIMMI: So maybe the cure is for me to say nothing? To stay silent?

BUNTY: You don't have to say a word! Even if you seal your mouth shut, a rapist can hear your thoughts! He'll know you're thinking, *PLEASE DON'T RAPE ME! PLEASE, PLEASE DON'T RAPE ME!* And that's all he needs. In order to rape you.

SFX: Applause.

NIMMI: All right. So there's no cure for the desire to rape. And there's no argument against a rapist's attack. So what's left? Deterrence?

BUNTY: (*laughs*) Deterrence! Hah.

NIMMI: You wouldn't laugh if you thought you'd get the death penalty each time you asked your question –

BUNTY: Greater the punishment, greater the charm!

SFX: Scattered applause.

BUNTY: And besides, which lawyer can face the fury of a rapist's MOTHER? An army of rabid she-wolves would be no match for *her*!

SFX: Applause.

After all, the mother of an accused rapist will defend her son's innocence with the last breath of her life – yes! – and she will tear the entrails out from the victim's entire clan and bathe in their blood before she'll allow one hair of her precious boy's head to be hurt!

SFX: Applause, roars, cheers.

NIMMI: Hmm. Funny you should say that.

BUNTY: Why?

NIMMI: Well. I have a son and a daughter. The girl's eighteen, the boy's twenty-two.

BUNTY: And? He's been accused of rape?

NIMMI: Huh! Never! How could he be? He's *my son*.

BUNTY: What – he's not manly enough to rape?

NIMMI: Shut up! Of course he's manly! He's handsome and smart and ... just ... *wonderful*. Nothing he ever does could be bad or wrong. So ... you're right! If some filthy slut tried to throw false accusations at him, I would definitely throw a US drone strike at *her*!

SFX: Applause.

BUNTY: (*he is amazed*) So ... so we're agreed?

NIMMI: Absolutely. You've totally convinced me – yes, yes, it's a great shame that rape causes agony to some women but unfortunately it *is* inevitable! Women can say "yes", "no" or "Humpty Dumpty" and they will *still* get raped, because that's our fate! There's nothing we can do except avoid it or enjoy it.

SFX: Applause.

And as you can hear, our audience agrees with us one hundred per cent too!

SFX: Applause.

Which is wonderful for ratings.

SFX: Applause.

BUNTY: What about your daughter?

NIMMI: What about her?

BUNTY: Don't you worry about her fate?

NIMMI: Not at all. I will just nail her to the bedroom wall until it's time for her to marry!

BUNTY: But what if ...

NIMMI: Nothing, nothing – she'll stay right there until we can find a rich man to be her husband. On her wedding night, he will of course force himself on her so that she can have an earth-shattering orgasm. After which she will have several hundred sons and be happy forever after. The end!

SFX: Roars, cheers.

I must say, I am really grateful to you, Mr Bunty, for clearing the cobwebs from our understanding of rape.

BUNTY: It's really all about culture, in the end.

NIMMI: Exactly! Here we were, thinking that rape is some criminal activity, when all along it's just as you say: *society loves rape!*

SFX: Applause, roars, cheers.

Because the fear of rape keeps women's sexuality in check!

SFX: Applause, roars, cheers.

And mothers shelter rapists ... *because one woman's rapist is another woman's blameless, innocent boy!*

And that's our show for tonight, ladies and gentlemen!

SFX: Applause, roars, cheers.

Thank you, Mr Bunty, for being with us tonight – thank you – thank you everybody – and goodnight!

SFX: Sustained applause, roars, cheers.

Lights fade out. SFX fade out.

Curtain.

BLIND DATE

At a table in a restaurant, conjoined female–male–female triplets ANNIE and BUDDY and CANDY are waiting to meet their blind date. ANNIE is on BUDDY's right, CANDY's on his left. They're dressed smartly but conservatively, with neatly styled hair, manicured hands, modest necklines, light make-up. They're attractive without being drop-dead. They have one pair of arms – that is, ANNIE has one right arm and CANDY has one left. BUDDY has no arms.

When the lights come on, ANNIE, BUDDY and CANDY are already seated, in what is clearly a secluded area of the restaurant. Muted sounds come from elsewhere, not directly around them. We do not see any restaurant staff.

CANDY: You know what I hate?

BUDDY: Yes. You've told us a thousand times.

CANDY: The hopelessness of it.

BUDDY: Conversation number five billion and eight ...

ANNIE: (*to CANDY*) Of what?

BUDDY: (*to ANNIE*) We KNOW what!

CANDY: Meeting mixed-gender conjoined triplets on a blind date.

ANNIE: Oh – *that*!

BUDDY: (*to CANDY*) *Why* d'you keep repeating it? WHY!

CANDY: It wasn't *my* idea. But triplets have no choice!

ANNIE: (*cutting in*) True, it was my idea, but false, you DO have a choice.

BUDDY: Oh no no no no no. Please, PLEASE ...

ANNIE: *Your* choice is to accept the inevitable and stop complaining.

BUDDY: I don't have fingers to stick in my ears!

CANDY: Or to keep complaining until one or both of you pays attention to me!

BUDDY: At least you're better off than me! You can block your ears if you want.

CANDY: Only my left ear.

BUDDY: That's better than neither!

ANNIE: Wrong again. You could use cotton in your right ear and your finger in your left. You could also cooperate with Buddy here and block HIS ears up too! If you wanted. But that's just the point. We've got this far in life by muddling along. By making do.

CANDY: Like I said: no choice.

ANNIE: No, the same as anyone else: we have choices that we choose not to ...

BUDDY: NO! You always, ALWAYS say that! And you're always, ALWAYS wrong. I have way less choice than all other men on earth!

ANNIE: Wrong! You could choose to see it as infinite access to two gorgeous ...

BUDDY: SISTERS! You call that choice? I call it self-abuse incest.

ANNIE: Two voluptuous bodies to ogle and feel up, whether or not they want to let you! That's more choice than most other men EVER HAVE!

BUDDY: (*bitterly*) As if! How can I feel anyone up? I don't have HANDS!

CANDY: Liar. You feel what we feel. When we feel ourselves up, you feel what we feel.

ANNIE: Both of us at once.

BUDDY: One hand at a time! Each one feeling up her own body! Separately and together ... together-ly! That's so surreal I can't even begin to describe what it's like.

ANNIE: You don't have to describe it. Not to us. We feel whatever you feel, but without your male brain attached. I think – I mean, seriously – it's quite magical.

CANDY: (*to BUDDY*) And what about your freedom from ... you know ... digestion end-products? You should be grateful you don't have a bum to clean!

BUDDY: Don't be ridiculous. It's not possible to feel grateful for an absence!

ANNIE: Of course it is. An absence of rain, for instance. An absence of pain. We can be grateful for those absences, surely?

BUDDY: I'm talking about experiences I've NOT had. Like body parts that other men have that I don't. How can I know whether or not I'm grateful? It would be like being grateful to be an atheist.

CANDY: What? No. That does NOT follow.

ANNIE: Believe me, you're grateful, whether you know it or not. Candy and I have to clean up the end-products of YOUR digestion mixed in with our own while you ...

BUDDY: NOT having a bum of my own is worse than having a bum that you don't want to clean. You forget, I can feel your hands cleaning your bums while I ...

CANDY: But what about the atheism? What did you mean by that?

BUDDY: I was referring to the classical argument about atheism. You know the one: by denying the existence of God, atheists affirm the existence of that-which-isn't-there.

CANDY: We were talking about bums, not God!

BUDDY: I can no more appreciate the lack of a bum I don't have than an atheist can appreciate the lack of a God that he – the atheist – claims does not exist!

CANDY: Huh. That's kinda ... cool. Never thought of bums and God in the same sentence before.

ANNIE: Okay, that's enough. We're going to keep the conversation clean from now on. No below-the-belt stuff.

CANDY: (*sighs*) I wonder if all conjoined triplets argue as much as we do.

BUDDY: This wasn't an argument, it was a discussion.

ANNIE: (*to BUDDY*) Oh, and by the way, just for your information, your breath DOES smell.

BUDDY: Oh, shut up! Being conjoined doesn't give you the right to make personal remarks!

CANDY: After all, being conjoined means sharing physical problems: too few hands, too many bums.

ANNIE: Being conjoined means never being alone with your breath. If you were alone, you'd check to see whether your breath smelled, wouldn't you? By holding your hand up in front of your mouth?

BUDDY: You *know* I can't do that –

ANNIE: Of course you can. When Candy's asleep, you can use her hand. I know, because I've seen you do it. I'm assuming you can use my hand too? When I'm asleep?

BUDDY: Well, I ... I ... (*clicks his tongue*) Anyway! It's not as if I can get both of you to fall asleep on demand!

CANDY: He certainly NEVER checks his breath! He's just like a singlet that way. Never worries about personal odours.

ANNIE: How can we know what singlets worry about? We have no idea what it's like being alone.

BUDDY: Aside from me.

ANNIE and CANDY: Shut up.

CANDY: Singlets don't bother with personal hygiene. Not really. They pretend to, but it's not the same as us. They don't have to. There's no sense in being considerate when you're alone. No one says "excuse me" when they burp alone in a room!

BUDDY: I do.

CANDY: That's coz you're NOT ALONE! (*exclaims under her breath*) *Jeez* ... (*takes out her pocket mirror, checks her hair*) Only a man would be so insensitive as to think he's alone even when HE'S CONJOINED!

BUDDY: A lone dog between two fightin' bitches.

ANNIE and CANDY: Shut up.

BUDDY: You see?

ANNIE: *We* see, you mean. And ... *we* mean. Being conjoined causes grammar to buckle and sway, ceasing to hold its form.

CANDY: Being conjoined would be awful even if we were all the same gender. But to be mixed gender and conjoined is ... ahh. Hateful. Grotesque. (*sudden change of mood, plumping up her hair*) How do I look?

BUDDY: Oh stop. They're going to hate us, whatever we look like! There's no point fussing with your hair –

CANDY: Everyone's not as prejudiced as you. I notice *you* got *your* hair done (*puts the mirror away*). Thanks to us, of course.

BUDDY: Can you blame me? It's all I have to offer – my face. My head. I would always get my hair done, even if I were going to my own execution. Our own execution. (*to ANNIE*) You never explained.

CANDY: Look, I have a request: just for the duration of this date, could we be separate individuals?

ANNIE: (*to BUDDY*) Explained what? And by the way, you have more than your head to offer.

BUDDY: (*to ANNIE*) Why did you take a decision to go on a blind date without consulting us? While we slept? As if we weren't part of your decision? (*to CANDY*) We ARE separate individuals. Sharing a conjoined fate. (*to ANNIE*) I hope you're not referring to my ... my ...

ANNIE: Your genitals. Yes. Of course that's what I'm referring to.

CANDY: I meant, could we use our own private pronouns? Just for this date.

BUDDY: (*to ANNIE*) What about keeping the conversation above the belt?

ANNIE: (*to CANDY*) I don't see how it matters. Using your own private pronouns isn't the same as having separation surgery. (*to BUDDY*) Because I'm the senior resident of this body. I was the first to draw breath. So. I'm the first to take decisions.

CANDY: I'm sorry, but it DOES matter. Like the toilet-seat controversy.

BUDDY: (*rolling his eyes up*) Oh. My. GOD! Don't start that up! Not now.

CANDY: (to *BUDDY*) But *you're* the one who complains! I never complain! Even though I'm the one who's inconvenienced!

ANNIE: We're BOTH inconvenienced –

BUDDY: (*to ANNIE*) It's useless arguing with her. Why d'you even try?

ANNIE: Because we're conjoined. We have no choice but to argue. Or else our heads would explode.

CANDY: I mean it: if you don't agree to using separate pronouns today I'll ... I'll ...

BUDDY: Go on! Say it, SAY IT!

CANDY: I'll refuse to deodorize your armpit.

BUDDY: Let the stink wars begin!

ANNIE: So then we'll all three be smelly. Remember? We can't get away from one another. If you don't deodorize my armpit, I won't deodorize yours.

BUDDY: It won't bother me. I'm a guy. Like you said, I don't notice body odours.

ANNIE: And anyway, it doesn't bother me. I'll buy a spray-on.

BUDDY: No! I *hate* spray-ons! And I can't block my nose!

CANDY: We'll have to go to the store together, remember? (*to BUDDY*) Why don't you shut up?

ANNIE: I'll order online.

CANDY: Oh, come *on*! You'll need both hands to type!

BUDDY: Why should I? Talking is all I *can* do.

ANNIE: Speak for yourself! I use Zen mail. (*to BUDDY*) Oh please! Who goes wee-wee all by himself? (*answering for him*) Haha. Certainly NOT you.

CANDY: What's Zen mail?

BUDDY: That's so SEXIST. That's so CRUEL! To use my anatomy to make fun of me.

ANNIE: The sound of one hand typing.

BUDDY: What?

ANNIE: Zen mail: the sound of one hand typing. (*to BUDDY*) For you, of course, it would be Buddy mail: the sound of no hand typing.

CANDY: Or, as the rest of the world calls it, "silence".

BUDDY: Are all singlets as cruel as either one of you?

CANDY: I suppose she thinks this is so funny. Well ... let her try just once to lace up her shoes without me!

ANNIE: I don't think it's funny. I'm no different from either of you. I hate every part of this. Of course I do. Waking up in the middle of the night, with both of you snoring! Feeling sick to think of a lifetime of unbearable togetherness.

CANDY: Toothpaste.

BUDDY: Butter-on-toast.

ANNIE: (*to BUDDY*) Whose side are you on? You can't afford to antagonize either of us! Why d'you keep doing it? But however much I hate it ...

BUDDY: Watch strap!

CANDY: Table tennis!

ANNIE: I still prefer to be alive than to be dead. (*to BUDDY*) Why! WHY do you bother to whine!

BUDDY: Because I can. It's the only thing I can do entirely on my own. Talk.

CANDY: Stop. Please, just STOP!

ANNIE: Anyway. That's the reason for this blind date.

CANDY: Which isn't going to happen. (*looks at her watch*) They're never going to come.

BUDDY: Maybe they're happy with one another. Maybe they're a set of three divinely self-realized souls!

CANDY: Wait! (*to ANNIE*) Say again? What's your reason? For the blind date?

ANNIE: To give us the chance to interact with people who aren't physically attached to us. To broaden our horizons. With others like ourselves.

BUDDY: We could have got that from three singlets too. Or even just one. Just one very caring soul.

CANDY: Ha. Singlets! We're just freaks for them. Not people.

ANNIE: Oh, they'll come all right! I set it up so that we'd be here ahead of time.

BUDDY and CANDY: What? (*pause*) WHY?

ANNIE: (*smiling*) Because I knew we'd need at least half an hour to argue about why we're here!

Offstage, muted clatter, voices, chairs being pushed aside suggesting patrons entering a restaurant.

CANDY: (*looking up*) Wait. Those sounds – is that them?

Enter stage left: EKS, WHY and ZEE, conjoined male–female–male triplets. EKS and ZEE are both big and burly. EKS has a shaven head, is covered in tattoos and has glittering face jewellery. ZEE is hirsute with a thick black beard and dreads. Their sister, WHY, wears heavy make-up and her hair is piled high on her head.

Their entire manner is loud. All their gestures, their movements, the way they fill space.

EKS: Hello, hello! Well! This is us! So we guess ...

ZEE: You must be you!

Raucous laughter as all three heads are thrown back in mirth.

ZEE: Buddy? Hey! How are you, man?

WHY: Shut up, you morons. (*addressing BUDDY*) Buddy! You have NO idea.

BUDDY: Uhh ...

ANNIE, BUDDY and CANDY slowly get to their feet. Not an easy task, as there are two pairs of feet involved.

WHY: My WHOLE LIFE I've been waiting to meet a guy like you.

ANNIE: (*tries to speak*) But he's not just a guy ...

EKS: (*doesn't acknowledge ANNIE*) So ... I guess you folks ... (*throws arms out wide, to take in the room*) you've just been sitting here waiting, huh?

ZEE: Man, it's DULL. Why don't we go someplace else?

WHY: (*she only addresses BUDDY*) Pay no attention to these worthless bums. They're just my brothers, you know? But we can be alone. Just you and me. (*to her brothers*) Let go the hands! Go on – LET GO THE HANDS!

EKS and ZEE let WHY use their arms to make her gestures.

ANNIE: (*trying to get a word in edgewise*) I must say ...

WHY: I guess you know how it is, right, Buddy? As the one in the middle, you get to call the shots, right?

ZEE: Yah. She does that.

EKS: Uses her voice. God.

WHY: (*to EKS and ZEE*) SHUT UP! (*to BUDDY*) Of course you do. I mean, you're also the man, right? So you probably have the best time. Me, I don't know. I have to really make myself HEARD. It's kinda boring, I can tell you, to be stuck between these two idiots –

EKS: Yup. We're idiots all right.

ZEE: We'd be lost without her!

EKS: Or ... anyway ... we'd be dumber. And maybe –

WHY: Pay no attention to them, okay, Buddy? They're so stupid they can't find their own dingdongs until I tell 'em how. But let's not hang about in this dump! It's so booooring. We've brought our van with us. Do you have transport? I mean, we got health services to pay for a customized vehicle made for us by BMW – free! Can you believe it? You better believe it!

ZEE: All because of her!

EKS: She's something else! We don't know where we'd be without her!

WHY: I mean, I've had guys come on to me just from the sound of my voice – like on the PHONE – I can get anyone to do *anything*! Just by the sound of my voice. I've had that gift from day one. I mean from *birth*. How about you? I'm guessing that maybe, as a *man*, you don't even *have* to say anything. Am I right? You're a guy, so you just get your way. Just by being a guy. Life isn't fair. It just isn't. I mean, look at me, stuck between two lunatics with their brains between their butt-cheeks. Seriously. It's disgusting. Do you have a butt? I mean, I don't, right?

EKS: (*with a leer*) But she has the OTHER thing!

ZEE: Oh yes, she does ...

WHY: And believe me, I know how to use it. But singlets? Ehhh. (*makes a disparaging sound*) I don't know. They're kind of dull. You know? They just don't get it, about being multiplets. The tragedy and the drama of it. I mean it's kind of hot too, right? I mean, with these two hunks on either side of me ... (*trails off seductively*)

ZEE: We take care of our girl, you know? Yes sir, we do. We look after her needs!

EKS: AND our own! Let's not forget our own, huh?

WHY: Only because I let them. Right, guys? I'm the one who taught you how to take turns.

EKS: Or else it's confusing, you know?

ZEE: Is that how it is for you too, Buddy? You get to take turns? You decide ... (*for the first time, he glances at ANNIE and CANDY as if noticing them properly for the first time*) ... right?

WHY: The one in the middle decides. It's the only obvious approach.

EKS: Or else she screams.

WHY: And I've got a voice. Like you wouldn't believe.

ZEE: Unbelievable. That voice.

WHY: Because the middle one has no other assets. So she's got to use the one she has. But you know that already, right?

You probably don't have to even raise your voice! You just whisper your needs. (*sighs*) Lucky guy.

ZEE: Are we going to leave or what? This place is getting me down.

ANNIE: (*raising her voice slightly*) I'm sorry, but I –

EKS: (*cuts in*) Coz I'm getting hungry, right? It's hard work, being a triplet. Keeping all of us fed.

WHY: C'mon. Let's go. We've got everything we need, in the van.

ANNIE: I'm sorry but I think we –

ZEE: It's not really a van. More like a kinda ...

EKS: Mobile home. That's what it is. A mobile home.

ANNIE: What's the matter with you?

WHY: C'mon. I'm ready. But we'll have a little fun before we eat, okay? Because I can tell ya, I'm pretty ravenous too. And I don't mean my mouth!

ZEE: (*lewdly*) Oh no, not her mouth!

EKS: So are ya coming, or what?

ANNIE: (*suddenly and very loud*) I'm SORRY! We're not going ANYWHERE!

EKS: (*surprised*) Excuse me?

WHY: (*haughtily*) I was talking to Buddy. It's very rude of you to interrupt, I must say!

CANDY: (*equally loud*) My sister's right. We're not going anywhere. Not with you.

WHY: (*raising her voice*) I was talking to BUDDY!

ANNIE: AND I WAS TALKING TO ALL OF YOU! (*her voice is louder than it's been so far*)

ZEE: (*shaking his head*) Uh-oh ...

EKS: Oh no, oh no ...

WHY: Wait – ARE YOU TRYING TO ...

ANNIE and CANDY: (*together*) OUTSHOUT YOU! YES! And guess what? THERE'S TWO OF US!

EKS: Shit, shit, shit ... (*hitting himself repeatedly on the forehead*)

ZEE: Lady, you do NOT want to do that! (*hitting himself repeatedly on the forehead*)

WHY: (*priming herself to scream*) You asked for it!

EKS: They asked for it ...

ZEE: (*plugging his left ear with his finger*) No, no – don't go there – don't –

WHY: (*opening her mouth wide, starting high*) AHHHHHHHHH ... (*the sound is stunning. Completely unnatural*)

CANDY picks up a glass of water from the table, leans forward and flings the water (only the water, not the glass) at WHY. Hits her full in the face.

WHY: (*begins to splutter*) ... akkk ... hackkk ... hackkk ...

EKS and ZEE: (*roaring together*) Aaaaarh! Aaaaarh! What did you do – quick, quick – she's choking! CHOKING!

They both thump her in the chest, struggling to coordinate all their reactions while WHY continues to choke and hack.

Lights start to fade over EKS, WHY and ZEE.

EKS and ZEE: (*together*) C'mon, let's get ourselves out of here! No time to lose, come on, come ON!

Their voices start to fade.

ANNIE: (*looking at CANDY, worried*) Candy! I think you might have ... maybe ...

BUDDY: (*cutting in*) It wasn't Candy! It was ME! I did that! Using Candy's hand!

EKS, WHY and ZEE fade out and exit.

ANNIE: You, Buddy?

CANDY: Wow. Good for you, Buddy. I guessed what you were doing and leaned forward.

BUDDY: I had to. I wasn't going to stand for that ... that ...

ANNIE: Bullying? Badgering?

BUDDY: I was going for "assault".

CANDY: But, Buddy ... she was, you know ... propositioning you! She wanted to ... to ...

BUDDY: I know. Fuck me.

ANNIE: Whups. Our little brother's all grown up!

BUDDY: I don't care. I hated her. Wouldn't fuck her if she was the last woman on earth. And we were singlets. And I was still a virgin.

CANDY: (*hushed*) Wow. Really, Buddy? All that?

BUDDY: What d'you think I AM?

ANNIE: A male slut. That's what you've always claimed. Always, always.

CANDY: I'm frankly amazed.

ANNIE: Me too.

BUDDY: Well, sure. I'm a slut. But not a GODZILLA-slut. Can you imagine what it might have been like?

ANNIE: Frankly, no.

BUDDY: Sheesh. A horror show. And their van? It sounds like a ... a ...

CANDY: Mobile boudoir?

BUDDY: I was going for "mobile abattoir"!

CANDY: As for the brothers!

BUDDY: Bizarre. Pitiful. Really. I pitied them.

CANDY: They seemed so big and tough!

BUDDY: But browbeaten. Like abused kittens. Puppet appendages to their tyrant sister.

CANDY: I'm so proud of you! I thought you'd be jealous of them.

BUDDY: Nah. No. I learnt something today.

CANDY: What?

BUDDY: That there are worse problems than my problem.

CANDY: Huh. Wow. That's a miracle. Coming from you.

BUDDY: We're not like them.

CANDY: My God. No! We're not.

BUDDY: I mean, we're ... well. I never realized how good-natured, calm and placid we really are. Never until today.

CANDY: It makes you think.

They both fall silent. Then both, without consultation, turn their heads towards ANNIE.

BUDDY and
CANDY: You're very silent.

CANDY: What're you thinking?

ANNIE: (*slowly*) I ... Well. It's hard to say it.

BUDDY: Is it something awful?

CANDY: Just spit it out, sis.

ANNIE: "Sis"! Huh. You never call me that!

BUDDY: Go on. Tell us.

CANDY: We can take it.

BUDDY: We have no choice, after all.

CANDY: Excuse me?

BUDDY: Well. Well! You know what I mean. We have a choice but we can choose not to exercise it ... oh come ON! Just tell us.

CANDY: Or don't. If you don't want to.

BUDDY: Oh, hey, hey! Are you crying?

CANDY: Oh my ... oh! Oh, don't cry, sweetie! *Please*!

BUDDY: If I had hands I would pat your back. Really I would.

ANNIE: I need a hanky.

CANDY: Here. Here's one –

ANNIE: (*breathing in short gasps*) It's just that I ... I ... wanted to say ... I LOVE you two. Us. I love us. (*sobs*)

CANDY: Oh! (*hiccups*) Oh – I ... (*reaching into her pocket*) Fortunately, I have two hankies.

ANNIE: Everything. Not just you as people. I mean, even being conjoined. I love that too. We're unique.

BUDDY: D'you mind hurrying up with that hanky? (*his voice breaks*)

CANDY: (*fresh sobs, as she turns towards him, to wipe his face*) Oh ... *Buddy*!

ANNIE: (*curling her arm around towards CANDY*) I love being unique.

CANDY: I hate it – (*sobs*) – and I love it!

BUDDY: My nose is running!

ANNIE: Group hug?

CANDY: (*laughing jerkily*) Not that we have a choice!

BUDDY: Heh. Here we go again!

ANNIE: We have a choice.

They are huddled together in a hug. Lights begin to fade.

ANNIE: That's the thing.

BUDDY: Please don't say it. My heart is bursting as it is.

CANDY: We love us.

ANNIE: Yes.

CANDY: We do.

BUDDY: I need the hanky.

ANNIE and
CANDY: (*together*) Shut up Buddy!

All laugh jerkily.

Lights fade out on their laughter.

Curtain.

ENDNOTE

There are, I believe three possible approaches to presenting a single set of multiplets: (A) three actors (B) two actors (C) one actor.

A: THREE ACTORS

Arrangement of limbs

The actor in the middle holds the actors on either side by the waist, while the two side-actors can decide how to arrange the hidden arm: either over or under the arm of the middle-actor. The two side-actors need to strap their right or left leg to (and behind) the adjacent leg of the middle-actor.

Clothes

The middle actor's clothes reflect his/her sex from the neck down, showing a complete body. The side-actors appear to have only one leg each and wear half-dresses or half-trousers, as the case may be.

Gender

Except for their voices, there's no need for the actors' actual sexual identity to reflect those of their characters in the multiplet. It would be highly desirable for the voices of the characters to reflect their different sexual identity.

Race

There's no need for the racial identities of the three different characters to match one another. I think it would be amusing to pair the two side-actors racially, but it would be equally effective if all three are different.

B: TWO ACTORS

Arrangement of limbs

The actor in the middle is represented by a fake head. The side-actors can take turns manipulating the head's movements by using their hidden arms. For the voice, they might use a recording, though in theory, they could also take turns using a deeper/higher voice to stand-in for the middle sibling.

Clothes

The middle character's clothes reflect his/her sex from the neck down, showing a complete body. The side-actors appear to have only one leg each and wear half-dresses or half-trousers, as the case may be. There needs to be a dummy torso between the two side-actors, in order to simulate the body of the third sibling between them.

Gender

As with (A) there's no need for the actors' actual sexual identity to reflect those of their characters in the multiplet, so long as the differences are clearly delineated.

Race

As with (A).

C: ONE ACTOR

Arrangement of limbs

A single actor plays the role of the middle sibling, with a dummy on either side, complete with heads. She/He would manipulate the single arms of either end characters. The legs would merely trail along on either side. The heads may need assistance from offstage puppeteers (from above?). A lot depends on the skill of the actor in the middle. If she/he is confident and dexterous, she/he might manage to get the heads to move by pulling strings.

Clothes

As with (A) and (B). However, the two dummies on either side need to be sturdily and cleverly made, especially if the heads are to be manipulated by the single actor.

Gender

The single actor's actual sexual identity matters very little. If she/he can do all three voices it would be great. Keeping their identities distinct would become a real challenge, however. My preference would be to use recorded voices for the side-characters.

Race

In this case, I think, it would be simpler, visually and conceptually, for all three siblings to match one another in race. Once again, though, it would depend on the skill of the single actor.

Introduction

The Organ Speaker

This is my "encore piece": a tiny amusement that I have never seen or heard performed in any sense. I wrote it in response to a request for a short performance piece, but it wasn't accepted.

As in so many other situations, rejections do not dent me! So here it is.

I always wanted to put together an audio file of the sounds required by the piece but didn't get around to it. Giant strides have been made in the business of creating sound libraries on the Internet. It takes an effort nevertheless, and a lot of time.

I am often told that my prose is "very visual". No doubt this is because of my parallel existence as an artist. What has never been remarked upon is the audio-dimension in my plays. Sound often plays a crucial role: the screaming in *Lights Out*, the electronic beeps of *The Mating Game Show*, the accents in *Harvest*, the audio-hallucination in *The Artist's Model.*

I have acute hearing, or used to, anyway, when I was younger. It means that I hear rather more than I want to. Irregular or intermittent sounds are like sandpaper applied directly to my eardrums. When I'm in a room with a ceiling fan I clip or weigh down loose papers to stop them from rustling. I prefer silence to any musical accompaniment when I'm working.

Favourite sounds include all the familiar ones: rain pattering on the window; a cat purring; the clickety-clack of a train at full speed; popping bubble wrap. And some oddities: the faint *tup* that comes from breaking the vacuum seal on the metal lid of a glass jar; the luxurious hiss of a heavy car's wheels on loose gravel; the tinkle of a silver straw in a tall glass of iced tea; the sound made by a single candle's flame on a cold night when the power has failed.

The echoing roar within a highly polished, iridescent nautilus shell.

THE ORGAN SPEAKER

Bare stage. A woman technician in a white lab coat enters, wheeling in an object which looks like a cross between a voltage stabilizer and an amplifier. Speakers reveal that it is some form of audio equipment.

TECHNICIAN:

(*she tinkers briefly before starting to talk*) Ladies and gentlemen, good evening and thank you for joining us here today. What you see before you is a piece of equipment called an Organ Speaker. As its name suggests, it is an instrument through which the organs of the human body – or ANY body, for that matter – can ... speak.

Perhaps some of you are wondering what led to the design of such an instrument? Well, the reason is simple. We refer to the organs of the body. And organs, we know, are also a type of musical instrument. So we – my fellow technicians and I – brought the two concepts together by adding a little electronic hardware, an amplifier, two speakers and a somewhat modified microphone. Instead of picking up sound waves, our mike picks up biorhythms.

By focusing and directing the microphone towards different parts of the body we were able to record not the mere audible sounds made by the body's various pipes and cisterns, but – how shall I put it? – the voice of the soul of these organs.

Think of it this way: our brain is an organ which has control over our lungs and our voice box. The result? We have audible speech.

But supposing that any of the other organs in our bodies had something to say, the stomach, for instance, or the heart – how would it express itself? We rarely notice our organs at all unless they scream at us by producing ulcers or heart attacks or lung cancer! We do not hear what they say unless they are in distress.

So! As I am about to demonstrate, with our machine, we have managed to change that.

To begin our demonstration, I am going to play for you the sounds recorded from the hearts of different people.

First we have ...

She switches on the machine at this point. It lights up, blinks and whirrs politely. From now on, each time she introduces an organ an appropriate sound will play.

... an average man's heart, healthy and at rest.

SFX: One pair of drumsticks on a snare drum – a simple uncomplicated rhythm, on and on.

Okay, and now we have a woman's heart, healthy and at rest.

SFX: Exactly the same sound.

Okay, and now we have the average man's heart when he sees the average woman.

SFX: Exactly the same sound.

Okay, and now we have the average woman's heart when she sees the average man.

SFX: Woman's voice calling in a high voice, "Dinner's ready!"

All right, and now we have the average man's heart when he sees a beautiful woman ...

SFX: Brief dramatic drum solo ending with crash of high hat.

... and here we have the average woman's heart when she sees a handsome man.

SFX: One pair of drumsticks on a snare drum – a simple uncomplicated rhythm, on and on.

Okay, and now we have the average woman's heart when she sees a handsome, sexy man.

SFX: One pair of drumsticks on a snare drum – a simple uncomplicated rhythm, on and on.

... and this is the average woman's heart when she sees a handsome, sexy and RICH man.

SFX: Sound of car accelerating, brakes – crash.

Okay! And now we have the NON-average man's heart when he sees a beautiful woman.

SFX: Fire alarm.

Okay! And now we have the NON-average man's heart when he sees a handsome, sexy man.

SFX: High whine of bomb falling through the air and exploding as it hits target.

... and the NON-average woman's heart when she sees a handsome, sexy and rich man.

SFX: Sound of snoring.

... and the NON-average woman's heart when she sees a handsome poet.

SFX: Opening bars of Richard Strauss's Thus Spake Zarathustra* *just until the drums.*

... and finally the NON-average woman's heart when she sees a beautiful FEMALE poet.

SFX: Sound of castanets.

All right! Now we're ready to move on to another organ. This time it's the stomach. All right, so to begin with, I'll play the sound of an average stomach at work.

SFX: Sound of washing machine on spin cycle.

Okay, and here's a hungry stomach.

* Just the "ta-daaaaaaaaaaaaaa!" before the drums.

SFX: Sound of dog snarling and barking.

Okay, and here's a teenager's hungry stomach.

SFX: Same sound of dog snarling and barking, but speeded up.

... and here's the sound of a kitty party's collective stomach just before lunch.

SFX: Sound of a team of Pomeranians yapping and yelping in high registers.

... and here's the sound of a business tycoon's hungry stomach.

SFX: Sound of lion roaring.

... and here's the business tycoon's HUSBAND's hungry stomach.

SFX: Sound of one Pomeranian yapping and yelping in high registers.

... and finally, here's a stomach after an Italian meal.

SFX: Dean Martin singing "O Solé Mio".

Okay! Moving along now – we go to ... the anus! This is an organ with a long history of abuse. Not only does it rarely see the light of day, it is almost never mentioned alongside its famous and highly sociable counterpart, the mouth. Well, I am glad to say, we have not ignored it. And so, for your benefit, here is the sound of your average, healthy, regularly functioning anus.

SFX: GONNGGGGGGGGGGGG!

Okay, and now we have an adult man's anus ...

SFX: Same GONNGGGGGGGGGGGG! but deeper.

... and this is an adult woman's anus ...

SFX: GONNGGGGGGGGGGGG! but higher.

... and this is a child's anus.

SFX: Pinggggggg!

Now we will hear a highly regular anus ...

SFX: Big Ben chiming the hour.

... and here's a less regular one ...

SFX: Cuckoo clock.

... an EXTREMELY irregular one ...

SFX: Fanfare from Thus Spake Zarathustra.*

... and finally, the once-a-year anus.

SFX: Deafening bomb blast.

All right! And that has us nicely warmed up. From the anus we pass smoothly on to the most vocal organs of all – the sex organs. Since these are significantly different for men, women and ... other creatures ... I will deal with each variety, separately.

First we will deal with the organs of men and ... other male beings. All right. Here we have the sound of a baby boy's organ, at rest.

SFX: Piccolo playing the scale.

Here is the sound of a young boy's organ, at rest.

SFX: Piccolo playing the scale.

Here is the sound of an adult man's organ, at rest ...

SFX: Piccolo playing the scale.

... and here is the sound of an adult man's organ, mildly aroused ...

SFX: Oboe playing the scale.

... and here is the sound of an adult man's organ fully aroused ...

SFX: Diesel truck horn.

* Just the "ta-daaaaaaaaaaaaaa!" before the drums.

Here is the sound of an adult man whose organ is facing a little difficulty.

SFX: Car with a dead battery.

Here is the sound of an adult man whose organ wakes at dawn.

SFX: Bugle playing reveille.

Here is the sound of an adult man whose organ has prodigious staying power ...

SFX: Ravel's Bolero.

... and an older man's organ fully aroused ...

SFX: Diesel truck horn.

... and a very old man's organ whenever he's awake ...

SFX: Diesel truck horn.

And now to different species. Here is the sound of a male garden shrew's organ when fully aroused.

SFX: Diesel truck horn.

Here is the sound of a male penguin's organ when fully aroused.

SFX: Diesel truck horn.

Here is the sound of a male polar bear's organ when fully aroused.

SFX: Diesel truck horn.

Here is the sound of a bull's organ when fully aroused ...

SFX: Diesel truck horn.

... and here is the sound of a male rabbit's organ when fully aroused.

SFX: Diesel locomotive at full throttle.

All right! And that brings us to the most vocal organ of all the organs on any body – the FEMALE sex organs. These organs have brought all of creation into being. These organs talk even when they have nothing to say and they keep on going, day and night, whether they are ignored or not, whether they are engaged in active conversation or not, whether we know they are there or not.

For the female sex organs, I am going to begin with a baby girl's organ.

SFX: Child's wind-up toy nursery rhyme – all tinkly-tinkly-tinkly sweet.

The pre-pubescent girl's organ.

SFX: Child's toy wind-up nursery rhyme.

The pubescent girl's organ.

SFX: Venga Boys.

The post-pubescent girl's organ.

SFX: Diesel truck horn.

Pre-marital virgin.

SFX: Child's wind-up toy nursery rhyme – all tinkly-tinkly-tinkly sweet.

Post-marital virgin.

SFX: Diesel truck horn.

Young mother.

SFX: Child's wind-up toy nursery rhyme – all tinkly-tinkly-tinkly sweet.

Young mother of twins.

SFX: Child's wind-up toy nursery rhyme – all tinkly-tinkly-tinkly sweet – at double speed.

Young mother of several small children.

SFX: Child's wind-up toy nursery rhyme – all tinkly-tinkly-tinkly sweet – at manic speed.

Different professional lives result in different sounds. Here is the sound of a door-to-door saleswoman.

SFX: Doorbell chimes.

A dotcom executive.

SFX: Dial-up networking sound.

A busy sex worker.

SFX: Cash register.

A doctor.

SFX: Ambulance wailing.

Opera singer.

SFX: Ambulance wailing with orchestral backup.

Bollywood actress ...

*SFX: Mallikarjun Mansur wailing with ambulance backup***

... and now we switch to the sounds made by the female sex organs of other species. However, we must point out that there is a difference between human females and the females of other species, which is that humans do not usually display the phenomenon of being "in season" or going "on heat" to the same extent as other creatures. Our recordings show that the female sex organs of other animals vocalize only during heat periods. So, here now is the sound of the sex organ of a female mouse during heat –

SFX: Lion roaring.

The organ of a female rabbit.

SFX: Lion roaring.

The organ of a female rhinoceros.

** Of course, we would never be able to get written permission for this! Substitute with sitar wailing.

SFX: Lion roaring.

The organ of a female three-toed sloth ...

SFX: Long pause, vague low-frequency sound – a lion roaring but at slow speed.

... which, when played at normal speeds is.

SFX: Lion roaring.

For our final selection we return to the sounds made by the sex organs of adult human females, but this time at different levels of satisfaction. First, we hear the sound of a perpetually dissatisfied organ ...

SFX: Cat wailing.

... then a mildly dissatisfied organ ...

SFX: A violin scale.

... and this is a satisfied organ.

SFX: A woman's voice singing a single note as in Hindustani classical music.

This is a reasonably well-satisfied organ.

SFX: A woman's voice singing a scale.

This is an extremely well-satisfied organ ...

SFX: Female opera singer approaching crescendo.

... and here now is the sound of an adult human female's sex organ at full satisfaction ...

SFX: The same female opera singer continuing.

... and climax.

SFX: Storm of concert audience applause as singer ends her song.

The applause continues as lights fade, technician bows, turns off the machine and exits. Cutain.

ACKNOWLEDGEMENTS

Given the number of plays, the length of time over which they were written and my extremely unreliable memory, it's very unlikely that this list will be anywhere near complete. What I have put down here represents the least, rather than the most, I can do to recall and thank those who have supported and encouraged me, or, in some important way, contributed to my work over the years.

The Rehearsal: Kim Pereira, professor of theatre, for agreeing to co-read with me in 2015 during my week-long residency at Illinois State University in Normal, Illinois, USA. Also, and separately, Alok Bhalla, critic, poet, author and retired professor of English literature, for publishing the piece as the guest editor of the 2010 winter issue of *Mānoa*, brought out by the University of Hawai'i, USA.

Hidden Fires: Jayant Kripalani for his warm insistence that I must complete the set of five monologues and his directorial support to get them performed; Naveen Kishore and Seagull Books for publishing them and for supporting performances of them. Alok Bhalla, critic, poet, author and retired professor of English literature, for publishing four of the *Hidden Fires* monologues as guest editor of the 2010 winter issue of *Mānoa*, brought out by the University of Hawai'i, USA.

Ladies' Night and *The Rape Artist*: Naveen Kishore and Megha Malhotra for giving me the opportunity to write these two short pieces during my stay in Kolkota as a guest of Seagull Books in 2013.

Blind Date: Shirley Houston-Findley for encouraging me to complete this odd and unlikely performance piece for her collection *Disparate Voices of Indian Women Playwrights*, 2019.

Thomas Abraham and Poulomi Chatterjee, my publishers at Hachette India for their patience and willingness to publish my work, including plays, which perhaps rank only after poetry as the least commercially viable form of literary publishing. Ansila Thomas for her willingness to struggle with me over the formatting nightmares caused by play scripts, OCR interpretations of published texts and the lack of standardization across the many different editions of my scripts. Bhavi Mehta for her always-outstanding cover designs.

Behind and beyond this constellation of friends and theatre lovers are, of course, my family: my sisters Geeta Doctor and Surya Narayanan, my nieces Meenakshi Doctor and Divya Narayanan, my nephew Vikram Doctor and also, always, Ethan Stein.

PUBLICATION HISTORY

The Rehearsal was first published in *Mānoa*, vol. 31 no. 2, p.120–125, University of Hawai'i, 2019. Republished in this edition with the permission of the author.

Hidden Fires (set) was first published by Seagull Books, 2003. Subsequently in *Mānoa*, vol, 22 no. 2, p. 73–96, University of Hawai'i, 2010. Republished in this edition with the permission of the author.

Blind Date was first published as part of *Disparate Voices of Indian Women Playwrights: Creating a Profession*, ed. Shirley Huston-Findley, p.141, London: Lexicon Books, 2019. Republished in this edition with the permission of the author.

The Sextet (set), *The Wish*, *The Senses-Taker*, *The Cook's Story*, *The Dhobi's Wife*, *Ladies' Night*, *The Rape Artist* and *The Organ Speaker* are all first published in this volume.

COLLECTED PLAYS
VOLUME ONE

BLOOD AND LAUGHTER

Plays

A neighbourhood that turns a blind eye to a recurring gruesome crime. A game show that puts the lives of its contestants on the line. An insidious tableau that pits three artists against each other. A world where organs of the poor are commercially harvested for the rich.

Collected Plays brings together, in a much-anticipated series, the dramatic works of Onassis Prize-winning playwright and author Manjula Padmanabhan.

Blood and Laughter, the first volume, presents within its covers Manjula's full-length plays – including the three-times-cinematized *Lights Out*, the previously unpublished *Mating Game Show* and *Artist's Model*, and the award-winning *Harvest* – all known for their masterful portrayal of the dilemmas of morality, relationships and the idea of justice. Horror, anticipation and chilling realism mark each of these works, drawing readers and audiences alike to the edge of their seats.

With new introductions to the works that affirm the relevance of the themes of the plays, this collection showcases the playwright's mastery of her art and reconfirms her standing among the leading dramatists of our time.

GETTING THERE

A young woman's quest for love, truth and weight-loss

Late 1970s, Bombay. Manjula is in her twenties, struggling to earn a living as an author-illustrator. Then, a deceptively routine visit to a diet clinic and an encounter with two tall Dutch men turn her life inside out.

Without much ado, she speeds off on a Westward-bound spiritual quest, which involves cheating on her boyfriend, lying to everyone she loves and cutting off all ties with her safe, respectable, bourgeois Indian upbringing.

In this picaresque travel memoir, novelist, cartoonist and award-winning playwright Manjula Padmanabhan looks back on her youthful misadventures in Europe. By turns funny and fierce, *Getting There* will touch anyone who has ever wanted to strip off their own skin to waltz, however briefly, on the wild side.

ESCAPE

In the country she inhabits, Meiji is unique. The only surviving female in a land where women have been exterminated, she has been brought up in secret, cloistered and protected, by three men she knows as her uncles - Eldest, Middle and Youngest. Now, as she approaches adolescence, her guardians must ensure that the dictatorial clone Generals who rule their world never get to know of her existence, and it falls to Youngest to escort Meiji on a long and treacherous journey through ravaged landscapes to the very edge of the world known to them.

An adventure story like no other, a tale of love and self-discovery in several unexpected layers, *Escape* is a novel that is as unsettling as it is unputdownable. In its captivating portrayal of tender relationships blooming and thriving in a vicious, forbidding landscape, it bears out Manjula Padmanabhan's genius as a creator of compelling alternative worlds.

THE ISLAND OF LOST GIRLS

This is the story of Meiji – the only girl who has remained untouched and unmutilated in a country that has savaged its entire female population. Having saved her from certain death in the new Dark Age that has come upon their homeland, her guardian, Youngest, has transported her to the only place where she can remain safe – an Island where wounded girls are, sometimes literally, stitched back together and given a new life.

But the Island itself is a menacing place, and Meiji may be in more danger than ever before. Now Youngest must find a way to infiltrate its odd environs to see what has become of his beloved girl, and escape once more…

The Island of Lost Girls showcases, yet again, Manjula Padmanabhan's genius at creating searing landscapes and alternate, sometimes brutal, worlds while reaffirming the beauty and the ugliness, the cruelty and the tremendous compassion, that essentially makes us human.

HARVEST

'A modern morality play. A bitter, savagely funny vision of the cannibalistic future that awaits the human race...' – *Outlook*

A searing portrayal of a society bereft of moral and spiritual anchors, Manjula Padmanabhan's fifth play, *Harvest*, won the Onassis Award for Original Theatrical Drama in 1997, the first year in which the prize was awarded. Following its international premiere in Greece in 1999, the play has been performed over the years by theatre groups, both amateur and professional, around the world.

A dark satire, *Harvest* tells the story of an impoverished family and the Faustian contract they enter into with a shadowy international corporation: fabulous wealth in exchange for the organs of one of its members. As Ginni, the glamorous American woman who hopes to receive the organs, invades their one-room home via an interactive video device the play lays bare the transactional nature of human relationships – even the most intimate ones.

This edition includes, for the first time, a gender-reversed version of the play – an experiment by the author that provides startling insights into the stereotypes and societal constructs ingrained deep in the human psyche and, indeed, into how we perceive gender.